Jim Britt's
Cracking the Rich Code[1]

Inspiring Stories, Insights and Strategies from Entrepreneurs Around the World

STAY IN TOUCH WITH JIM, KEVIN AND JOEL

For daily strategies and insights from top entrepreneurs, join us at

THE RICH CODE CLUB

FREE members site.

www.TheRichCodeClub.com

Co-authors From Around the World

Jim Britt

Kevin Harrington

Joel Sauceda

Carla Walker

Knicole Burchett

Beth Robins

Merrilee Sweeney

Missy Grohne

Mark Recker

Jason J Volpe

Norm Dupas

Phil Bristol

Dr Yvonne Oswald

Charol Messenger

Rylee Meek

Tamara Paul

Roxanne Tuomela

Mache Torres

Joy Gilfilen

Christian Fea

Jeffrey Flack

Karl Roller

DEDICATION

Entrepreneurs will change the world, they always have and they always will.

To the entrepreneurial spirit that lives within each of us.

Foreword by Kevin Harrington

You probably know me as one of the "Sharks" on the hit TV show Shark Tank, where I was an investor in many entrepreneurial ventures.

But my life and business wasn't always like that. I used to be your regular, everyday guy patching cracked driveways to make money. I had hopes and dreams just like most, yet I worked around people who didn't support my dreams. But you know what? I not only found a way out, but I found a way to my dreams... and so can you.

Now, I wake up every morning excited about my day, and I surround with only the people I want in my life; entrepreneurs who really want something more than just getting by paycheck to paycheck.

Today we hear stories -- mostly from the mainstream media -- everyday about how bad things are, businesses are closing and jobs being lost, interest rates are on the rise, how the gap between rich and poor is growing and how you'll never make it on your own.

But here's what I know for sure. Entrepreneurs are going to change the world. We always have and we always will.

Forget the 1% vs the 99%. 100% of us entrepreneurs need answers. We need solutions. We need something more than what we're being told by those who don't have a clue. We need to start saying Yes! to opportunity and No! to all the noise.

The fact is that it's a new world and a new economy. The "proven" methods of doing business and investing that produced successful results, even two years ago, simply may not work anymore.

If you want to succeed (or even survive) in our new world, you need an entirely new set of skills and information.

You need to "reposition" yourself…often.

You need to revamp how you do business…often.

You need to change how you handle and invest your money…often.

Like any other situation, if you know WHAT to do and WHEN to do it, you'll not only be "safe"... you could easily skyrocket financially.

If you have the right knowledge for today, the right opportunities for today, the right strategies for today and most of all the right character and mindset for today, you can win — and you can win big!

What I've discovered in my over three-decade career as an entrepreneur, is that success in the face of financial adversity boils down to 3 things:

The right knowledge at the right time.

The right opportunities at the right time.

The right you... ALL the time.

The bottom line is this: you can no longer afford to rely on anyone else to navigate your financial future. You have to rely on your "self." The question is... do you have a "self" you can rely on? Unfortunately, when it comes to entrepreneurship and money, many people don't. They don't have the financial education, the mental toughness, the knowledge and the skills to build wealth... especially in an ever-changing marketplace. You need to get RE-educated. You need to REINVENT yourself for success in the new economy. You need to learn new strategies in the areas of business and career, finance and real estate that create wealth or at least financial freedom in today's new world. But that's not all...

Skills and strategies and all that profound new knowledge won't do you one bit of good if you don't have the CHARACTER, the HABITS and the MENTALITY it takes to get rich. If you have internal barriers, your road to success will be slow and full of pain and struggle. It's like driving with one foot on the gas and one foot on the brake and always wondering why you aren't getting anywhere. Your mind is working against you instead of for you.

I have seen business owners come to me with their business ready to go under — and have the next year be their best financial year ever. I've see others that had a business that should skyrocket, yet fail because they didn't have the mental toughness to go the distance. I have seen people stuck in dead-end, dreary jobs break out of their rut, get involved in a brand-new passion, and become wildly successful.

No matter what you do for a living...regardless of your education, level of business experience or current financial status...If you have a burning desire for financial change then you won't want to miss this rare opportunity to learn from the entrepreneurs within this book.

It will provide you with some of the same success strategies that Jim Britt and I have used personally and shared with tens of thousands of people who've had tremendous financial success...people just like you, who wanted to get out of the rat race and enjoy financial freedom.

In addition, you'll learn what others have done, mistakes they made and how you can avoid them. You'll discover strategies that could make your business into a major market leader. I always say "Just one good idea can change everything."

Success is predictable if you know what determines it. This book offers some valuable tips, knowledge, insights, skill sets, that will challenge you to leap beyond your current comfort level. If you want to strengthen your life, your business and your effectiveness overall, you'll discover a great friend in this book. You'll probably want to recommend it to all your entrepreneurial friends.

Although I haven't followed Jim Britt's career over the last 40 years, but I do know that he is recognized as one of the top thought leaders in the world, helping millions of people create prosperous lives. He has authored 13 books and multiple programs showing people how to understand their hidden abilities to do more, become more and enjoy more in every area of life. I also want to recognize Joel Sauceda, our online business partner. He is the brains behind the many online PR, Marketing, Branding and Lead Generation strategies each entrepreneur coauthor and reader of the book will benefit from.

The principles, concepts and ideas within this book are sometimes simple, but can be profound to a person who is ready for that perfect message at the right time and is willing to take action to change. Maybe for one it's a chapter on leadership or mindset. For the next, it's a chapter on raising capital, or securing a business loan. Each chapter is like opening a surprise empowering gift.

The conclusion to me is an exciting one. You, me and every other human being are shaping our brains and bodies by our attitude, the decisions we make, the intentions we hold and the actions we take daily. Why is it exciting? Because we are in control of all these things and we can change as long as we have the intention, willingness and commitment to look inside, take charge of our lives and make the changes.

I want to congratulate Jim Britt for making this publication series available and for allowing me to write the foreword, a chapter in each book and be involved with the entrepreneurs within this book and series. I honor Jim and the coauthors within this book and the series for the lives they are changing.

As you enter these pages, do so slowly and with an open mind. Savor the wisdom you discover here, and then with interest and curiosity discover what rings true for you, and then take action toward the life you want.

So many people settle for less in life, but I can tell you from my experience that it doesn't have to be that way.

Be prepared…because your life and business is about to change!

Jim Britt & Kevin Harrington

As co-creators of this book series Jim Britt and Kevin Harrington have devoted their lives to helping others to live a more prosperous, fulfilled and happy life. Over the years they have influenced millions of lives through their coaching, mentoring, business strategies and leading by example. They are committed to never ending self-improvement and an inspiration to all they touch. They are both a true example that all things are possible. If you get a chance to work with Kevin and Jim or becoming a coauthor in a future Cracking the Rich Code book, jump at the chance!

Table of Contents

Cracking the Rich Code[1]

Jim Britt

Jim Britt is an internationally recognized leader in the field of peak performance and personal empowerment training. He is author of 13 best-selling books, including *Cracking the Rich Code; Cracking the Life Code; Rings of Truth; The Power of Letting Go; Freedom; Unleashing Your Authentic Power; Do This. Get Rich-For Entrepreneurs; The Flaw in The Law of Attraction;* and *The Law of Realization,* to name a few. He is co-creator of 16 volume "The Change" book series.

Jim has presented seminars throughout the world sharing his success principles and life-enhancing realizations with thousands of audiences, totaling over 1,500,000 people from all walks of life.

Jim has served as a success counselor to over 300 corporations worldwide. He was recently named as one of the world's top 20 success coaches and presented with the best of the best award out of the top 100 contributors of all time to the direct selling industry.

Jim is more than aware of the challenges we all face in making adaptive changes for a sustainable future.

The Predator and the Prey

By Jim Britt

Maybe you have dreams and goals, but somehow things are simply not moving in the direction you had planned? Or worse, maybe you've stopped believing that the life you've always wanted is even attainable?

Let me ask you. Do you see similarities between you and your parents? The reality is that DNA passes down through generations… you, your parents, grandparents, great-grandparents, and so on. You could actually track it right back to when your ancestors lived in a cave. And in order to survive, prehistoric man needed to be able to see an event and interpret it as danger or safe…immediately! They had two dominant thoughts, "kill something to eat" and "keep from being killed and eaten." And to some degree, we still have this mechanism of recognition in place today. We just don't view it the same way.

Something happens… and your brain stretches and searches all through your past networks… or dendrites, which are the memory channels woven throughout your DNA looking to match some sort of pattern so you can make an instant decision… is this safe or dangerous? The meaning you give something is based upon a constant comparison of your past experiences and DNA programming projected into the future with the anticipation or possibility of it happening again. Something happens and you immediately tell yourself a story about what it means. Remember, it's a made-up story in your mind. It's not real… yet.

So when you step into the future, you don't really step into an empty future, but rather into a future that is filled with interpretations about what happened in the past, and what could happen in the future if you proceed.

For example, a salesperson prepares her presentation. She is excited for that important appointment to make a sale, but instead of a sale she gets a very rude "no." Now the next presentation, she won't step into a blank future, but rather, first, she steps into a previous negative past experience. Put enough of these "no's" together and now the salesperson does everything in her power to avoid prospecting so she doesn't have to experience another 'no.' Again, the rejection had no meaning until she gave it one. She got a "no" and she made it mean something about her, when in reality it wasn't about her at all.

Imagine three circles. A circle on the left. In that circle something happens to you... broken marriage, lose money in a business venture. You decide what goes in there.

Now there's the circle on the right. This is where you gave what happened to you meaning. Examples...bad experience with last business. Business didn't work last time and may not work now. Marriage ended in divorce. I don't want that again. You gave whatever happened to you a meaning.

Now, the circle on bottom. You live your life as if your story is true. We live in a black and white world.

However, most live their life in the gray as if their story is true, when in reality, it's a made-up story created from past experiences. This is an example of inauthentic living. You are living as if your story is true and reacting accordingly. Everyone has a story, but the reality is that your story is in large part an illusion... it's a made-up belief. All beliefs are false until you decide they are true, but that doesn't make them true. But if you decide it is true, then it will be true for you.

Core beliefs work like sunglasses. Sunglasses change incoming light before it hits our eyes. The world does not change to a shaded image just because you put on sunglasses. Only your perception changes looking through the glasses. Wear sunglasses long enough and you will eventually forget you have them on.

That's how beliefs work as well. Believe something long enough and eventually you experience it as true. It then becomes a core belief. Core beliefs change how you see the world before you are even aware of seeing anything. And core beliefs also determine how the world sees you. That's right. The world sees you the way you see you.

On the other hand, this mechanism is critical for your survival because it separates things that might get you killed and eaten from everything else. In a sense, your core beliefs protect you. But not always, because you automatically filter everything that happens to you according to core beliefs, which may or may not be true. In other words, your core beliefs may not be taking you in the direction you want to go.

Prey animals cannot afford to not follow their core beliefs. Humans are no exception. The top priority our brains have is to keep us from getting killed and eaten...maybe not literally in today's world. But, you may fear getting killed and eaten by an audience when you step on a stage, or by a prospect when making a presentation.

These things represent predators waiting to invade your refuge and attack you if you leave yourself open, or you start to take a risk. Our brains are wired to fear monsters, noises, and dangerous situations, because that is what our ancestors had to do to survive.

Humans of all ages establish and stick to routines no matter what, so they can survive. We take comfort in our routines. This makes perfect sense.

For example, if a predator attacks at dusk, then its prey should be out and about during the day and asleep and out of reach at night. If a predator attacks at noon, then the prey would most likely be nocturnal. Sticking to this routine helps the prey stay alive. Our prey habits are all about avoiding predators, discomfort, or dangerous situations.

Humans are prey animals whose top priority is not getting killed and eaten, avoiding pain, or not getting hurt. We therefore form habits to help us survive and then stick to those habits no matter how inconvenient, uncomfortable, unrealistic, or awful they are. We learned over countless generations that straying from our routine puts us at risk. Our brain does everything in its power to keep that from happening. This is why people refuse to change until the pain of *not* changing is worse than the pain of changing.

We desire to change, but when faced with the pain of change we weigh out both sides—the pain of staying where we are and the pain associated with changing. Whatever causes us less pain is what wins out. But the question is, do you win, or do you continue living a life of more of the same?

Core beliefs form our entire reality from birth to death unless we take action to change them. The good news is that you can change your beliefs. We do it all the time. Remember, a belief is a made-up story. Want to change it, make up something new!

It's like earning a six-figure income for example. Once you hit it, it becomes a core belief, so you settle for nothing less. The catch is that changing your beliefs will force you to confront programming that your brain interprets as being essential for your very survival. This is why crash diets, New Year's resolutions, joining a gym, opening a savings account, cutting up the credit cards, and other drastic changes rarely last more than a few days to a few weeks. At some point, the desire for change surrenders to the brain's built-in attempts to keep you from getting killed and eaten.

How do you change a core belief? Make up something new, let go of all that doesn't support it, and stick to it until it becomes a core belief.

Remember, every life level requires a different you. Think about that…EVERY LIFE LEVEL REQUIRES A DIFFERENT YOU.

Just look at your own life. What are some examples of drastic changes you have attempted in your own life?

Change requires that you change your perceptions.

Imagine a gopher that hides from hungry birds during the day. Most gophers will not leave their burrows during the day unless some emergency happens. For example, flooding the burrow gives the gopher the choice of *certain* death by drowning or *possible* death by escaping. In this example, the risk of following the normal routine becomes greater than the risk of doing something different.

Humans work the same way, except that our fears are based on past experiences combined with future anticipations. These fears are not real. They are imagined. They are a made-up story based on past experiences and programming that are designed to keep us safe. Just like the gopher, we weigh out the pain of staying where we are, not taking a risk, staying where we are comfortable, versus doing something in a different way.

Our routines form what's known as our comfort zone. We refer to doing things we don't normally do as "leaving the comfort zone." How did you feel the last time you left your comfort zone? Maybe someone asked you to deliver a short speech to a group of your peers. You may have felt scared, nervous, insecure, and ready to bolt at a moment's notice. This is a perfect example of our prey instincts telling us to get back in our comfort zone as quickly as possible.

I remember my first experience speaking. I literally thought I would be killed and eaten! I was to speak for 20 minutes to a group of about 20 people. I prepared for a month. I must have written 20 pages of notes. I couldn't stop thinking about it. What might happen if I didn't do it right, or forgot what I was supposed to say, or I might say it wrong, make a mistake…the list was endless.

I was staying in a hotel the night before I was to speak. I couldn't sleep, for fear of being killed and eaten! I tried to think of ways I could get out of speaking. Nothing seemed to make any sense. Then I came up with the answer. I will have an accident on the way to the speaking engagement. Not a huge one. Just something small, but big enough that I could show my bent fender so it looked legit. I figured the accident would be less painful than speaking.

Just as I went for the door to leave for my accident, someone knocked. I thought it was probably housekeeping, so I opened the door. It wasn't housekeeping. It was my associate that had booked the speaking engagement for me. He said, "I came to pick you up." My first thought was "you are going to be in an accident."

I said, "I'll drive."

He said, "No I'll drive."

I said, "No I want to drive."

He said, "I'm parked in front of the door. I'm driving."

I thought, "Do I grab the wheel of his car and have an accident?" I decided not to do that, but to follow through with the speech.

We arrived. I felt like I wanted to throw up. I was terrified. I took a few deep breaths and started my talk. I spoke for 20 minutes and I have no idea what I said. When I finished, I immediately went outside and stood beside the car and did a lot of deep breathing to regain my composure.

"Never again" was what I was thinking. After a few moments, I thought, "I have one of two choices. Never do it again, or do it often until I got better at it." After a lot of mental back and forth, I chose the latter.

I was in charge of about 300 salespeople that did presentations for small to medium sized groups to sell seminar tickets for a Jim Rohn seminar. I put the word out that I was available to do up to three presentations a day to groups of fifty or more…which I did for the next five years. And after about 15 presentations a week, almost 3500 total, I finally lost my fear of being killed and eaten by an audience. I created a new belief, a program that was stronger that the old one.

The stronger the urge to get back to your comfort zone increases, the farther you stray. This happens because our brains are wired to learn and follow habits designed to keep us safe and alive. We do this by learning how our predators behave and then creating patterns to avoid them, even if our predators only exist in our imagination. Like the "no" that the salesperson gets over and over, until now they are afraid to even prospect. The "no" becomes the predator.

Like the person that has been hurt multiple times in a relationship. And now the thought of getting involved in another relationship becomes very scary.

The comfort zone is nothing more or less than behavioral boundaries set by your core beliefs that were either formed when you were too young to understand what was happening, or over a long period of time through repeated experiences.

Core beliefs form your entire reality from birth to death unless you take action to change them. The good news is that you can change your beliefs. We do it all the time. Just think of something you used to believe that you no longer believe. Do you still believe what you believed in high school? Once you got out into the real world, you most likely looked back and laughed at some of the stupid things you did and what you believed to be true and realized it wasn't true at all.

It's like earning a six-figure income for example. Once you hit it, if that's the case, now you believe you can, so you settle for nothing less. That's called creating a new belief. The catch is that changing your beliefs will force you to confront programming that your brain interprets as being essential for your very survival.

Again, this is why crash diets, New Year's resolutions, joining a gym, opening a savings account, cutting up the credit cards, and other drastic changes rarely last more than a few days to a few weeks. At some point, the desire for change surrenders to the brain's built-in attempts to keep you from getting killed and eaten, unless you decide and commit to experiencing the pain of change and you stick with it until you change.

Just look at your own life. What are some examples of drastic changes you have attempted in your own life? How have they worked out for you?

How can you change when you run up against instincts designed to keep you safe and alive? A prey animal needs to react to predators without question. And if you want change, you have to become self-observant to determine what you should act upon and what is old programming that no longer serves your greater good.

Indecision causes hesitation. And if you hesitate, you could get killed and eaten! Hesitation gives predators an extra split second to move in for the kill.

It's starts with a decision to change whatever it is you want to change. So when one of those old programs arise, stop! Stop like you approach a red light at a busy intersection with a sign that reads "right turn on red after stop." Stop and ask yourself. "If I proceed, will this take me in the direction I want to go? Is this fear real or in my imagination, based on old programming?"

Take a good look at any animal whose parents raise the young. The young stick around to learn the survival skills they need to stay alive. Prey animals learn when they can come out, where to go, how to avoid predators, and when to retreat back home. Their survival depends on absorbing this information and mastering the skills without question. We were taught similar things. "That's hot, don't touch that, you'll go blind." "Careful, you'll fall."

Of course certain things we have learned have become essential to our survival. But unlike prey animals, we humans are programming our young from birth till they leave home, good or bad, right or wrong.

We are programmed about money based on how rich or poor our parents were and how they handled money. We were programmed about relationships, good or bad, based upon our parents' relationship. We were programmed regarding our eating habits, how we think, attitudes, and so on…good or bad.

Again all beliefs are false, until we decide they are true. The dictionary defines belief as, "to hold an opinion." We are programmed and convinced that our beliefs are true, whether they are true or not. In other words, we see and experience our beliefs as true. Two plus two equals four because we believe it does. If you believe that two plus two equals five, then no amount of argument will convince you otherwise, unless you choose to change that belief.

Beliefs equal truth because they are the mental sunglasses that filer your senses before you perceive the sensation. Your reticular activating system selects which sensory input is important based on your beliefs. Change a belief, and your view of the world changes, as well as the view others have of you.

Your beliefs color every bit of the input you receive. Only when you believe something do you become aware of the sensation of the input.

If our personal reality is based on core beliefs, then the universe that each of us experiences is not the cause but rather the effect of whatever is left over after our core beliefs do their work.

The statement, "I'll believe it when I see it" is backward. We actually see things *because* we believe them.

This has some amazing implications when you start to look at life in this way. Think about it. We see things *because* we believe it. Back to what I said earlier. When you change a belief, your view of the world changes.

So what is the answer to changing? The answer, or rather the challenge, is to take the negative past out of the present. The real goal should be to have your present empty of the negative past, and not to give the past meaning unless you say so.

Self-observation is the key.

Is what I'm giving energy right now taking me where I want to go? Is this fear or conflict supportive or non-supportive? Bottom line— is it true, or is it something you have been programmed to believe is true?

To change a belief, you have to challenge it.

Is it true?

What experience do you have that makes it true?

How do you know it to be true?

Who taught you to believe this?

What if they didn't know?

What if it's not true?

Who would you be without this belief?

What action should I take next?

When you achieve this level of control, you will experience what is known as true emotional freedom.

You'll have the freedom to choose fascination over frustration, success over failure, calm over upset.

When you take responsibility and observe reality… in other words what's really happening, you can then choose to create whatever reality you want.

Start today, by identifying a story you have been telling yourself that has been holding you back in life.

I can't get ahead financially. That's a story, not reality. It is not true unless you say it is.

I can't seem to keep a relationship together…

It's hard to lose weight…

Pick a story, just one to start. Look for the truth, then take action based upon that truth. The question is, does your interpretation of this story serve you or hold you back? Notice what you say to yourself about what has happened, and then exercise the freedom to choose a different interpretation.

I don't want you to believe me. I want you to try it and experience the result for yourself. You'll experience a positive result the very first time you try it.

Hey, and watch out for those predators!

***

To contact Jim:

www.JimBritt.com

www.LiveLifeAtLevelTen.com

www.TheRichCodeClub.com

www.PowerOfLettingGo.com

www.jimbrittbook.com

www.CrackingTheRichCode.com

www.FaceBook.com/JimBrittOnline

www.linkedin.com/in/jim-britt

Kevin Harrington

Kevin Harrington is an original shark from the hit TV show *Shark Tank* and a successful entrepreneur for more than forty years. He's the co-founding board member of the Entrepreneurs' Organization and co-founder of the Electronic Retailing Association. He also invented the infomercial. He helped make "But wait... There's more!" part of our cultural history. He's one of the pioneers behind the *As Seen on TV* brand, has heard more than 50,000 pitches, and launched more than 500 products generating more than $5 Billion in global sales. Twenty of his companies have generated more than $100 million in revenue each. He's also the founder of the *Secrets of Closing the Sale Master Class* inspired by the Master of sales—Zig Ziglar. He's the author of several bestselling books including *Act Now: How I Turn Ideas into Million Dollar Products, Key Person of Influence,* and *Put a Shark in Your Tank.*

Becoming A KPI

By Kevin Harrington

The Key Person of Influence (KPI) in any given industry is the leader. It is the leader of the business world, the leader of automobile dealerships, the leader of selling hats—you name it. In other words, being the KPI means being the go-to person. The crazy thing? Anyone can be a Key Person of Influence. Any entrepreneur can be a KPI, a doctor, a salesperson, anyone. Just follow five steps and you will be well on your way. What comes with being a Key Person of Influence is value, ideally a massive amount of money, and being the leader in your field. The KPI is the person who comes up in conversations when it relates to a certain product, business, company, industry, or field. This is the person others seek out, the go-to person. Being the Key Person of Influence is how I got on *Shark Tank*.

Here's the story: I got a phone call from Mark Burnett's company. Mark Burnett is a television producer. He produced shows like *Survivor* and *The Voice*. His office called to set up an appointment. Mark was starting up a new show and wanted me to go out to Los Angeles to talk business. I was curious as to how Mark Burnett's company found me, and why they reached out for my services. They told me it was because I was a Key Person of Influence. I was all over the internet as a result of everything I was doing. It was 2008, and I had been in the business for 25 years. I had created huge brands. I helped build Tony Little. I helped build Jack Lalanne. I helped build Food Saver. We did the NuWave Oven. We worked with people like George Foreman and countless others. The problem was, everybody knew the brands, which was good for business, but did nothing for my personal brand. Consumers knew about the Food Saver, they knew about Tony Little, and they knew about Jack Lalanne, but not everyone knew I was the guy behind all of these people. Nobody knew me.

At that point, I made a conscious effort to build my brand. I wanted to become the go-to person so I could get the hot products and the phone calls. I helped build Tony Little's business, but everyone called him; they weren't calling me. What's wrong with that picture? Well, for one, I invested millions and millions of dollars of my own capital into Tony Little, and then he got all the phone calls. Shame on me for doing that, right? So I decided to build my brand, and that's when I came out with my book, *Key Person of Influence*. I promoted myself by doing radio talk shows, TV shows, trade journals, speeches, etc. This is how I got on *Shark Tank*.

If I hadn't met Daniel Priestley, my book could have become *How To Become The Go-To Guy* because that's what I was looking to do, but Daniel very eloquently created this five-step system called the "Key Person of Influence." Realizing we were on to something, we co-authored and launched *Key Person of Influence*. Let's look now at the necessary steps to become a KPI.

Obtaining Customers

In 1984, I started a business of obtaining customers on TV. One evening, I was watching the Discovery Channel and suddenly the channel went dark for about six hours. I then called the cable company just in case there was a problem. They told me there wasn't a problem, that the Discovery Channel was an 18-hour network. That's when the light bulb went off. This was downtime. They put no value on those six down hours. Instead of showing something during this time, bars were put up on the screen. I started thinking about what I could put in place of that downtime, to sell something, obtain customers, and make money. I'm like the Rembrandt TV guy. I created and invented the whole concept of going to TV stations and buying huge blocks of remnant downtime. In all these years of me doing this, no one has challenged the idea that I was the person who did it, created it, and invented 30-minute infomercial blocks.

I was buying big blocks of time. Why? Because I wanted to obtain customers. How do you obtain customers? A lot of ways, but you ultimately have to get some form of media. How does it start? There are two metrics you have to look at when obtaining customers. What does it cost to obtain the customer? That is called the Cost Per Order (CPO). What is your Average Lifetime Revenue Value (ALRV), or Average Order Value (AOV)? The cost to obtain the customer obviously has to be less than the cost you are going to receive in income from the customer. The bottom line in obtaining customers: you have to set up a system. You have to set up testing. You have to set up as many sources for obtaining customers as possible. Even though I was in the TV business, I didn't just get customers through TV. Customers came through TV, radio, the internet, retail stores, international distribution, home shopping channels, etc. The first step is to make a laundry list of every possible resource for attracting these customers.

Today, some people who are into the digital space are basically just getting customers on the internet. Some of the areas I mentioned above have become very expensive. It's tougher to make money on TV. While we started on TV, the cost to get customers has become too high; so we now have made the switch to digital. When you talk about internet, there's many different ways to obtain customers, from Google AdWords to Facebook ads to social media, etc. You can also attain customers with public relations and influencers. You have to decide what works best with your product. The bottom line, is a lot of people do not realize they have to be sophisticated, from a business analysis standpoint, to set up a business. You need a marketing plan to obtain customers.

First, focus on two numbers: your Customer Acquisition Cost (CAT) and Average Order Value (AOV). Those numbers have to work. Customer service is crucial in the business world as well. A business can't have bad customer service and retain customers This is especially true in this day-and-age.

Raising Capital

I had a 50-million-dollar-a-year business, making $5 million a year in profit. Feeling confident, I met with seven banks to get some financing. I thought it was going to be easy because I had a very profitable business. Unfortunately, bank after bank after bank turned me down. I had great credit and all of that. The only asset I had was the business. Part of the problem was I didn't know how to approach the banks. I was a young entrepreneur in my twenties. I had no real credibility in the banking world; I was walking in and just showing my numbers from the year before.

So what did I do to get the capital? Well, I ran into a mentor who was a former bank president, and he said, "Kevin, you went about it all wrong. I come from the banking business, and if you walked into my office and said, 'I need 5 million bucks,' I would have told you to turn around and get the hell out of my office. What do you have to do? You have to sell them on the future. What you did last year is well and good, but they are giving you money because they know that you are still going to be in business three years from now repaying their loans. You need projections. You need your forward business plan. You need your five-year master plan. You need to talk the talk and walk the walk, otherwise they aren't even interested."

I hired my mentor as a consultant to the company. I brought him in on the ground floor as part of my dream team. To make a long story short, we went back to re-pitch some of the same banks. We didn't get 5 million dollars, but we got a 3-million-dollar line of credit. It was all in how we talked to the banks. We had the same business, but it was all in the presentation. It's all in how you talk and how prepared you are. Raising capital is mental. It's in the pitch. It's in the relationships you build, etc.

One of the biggest challenges with any business is having enough capital to do the things you want to do. You have to have a successful business plan if you want to raise money. Here are the elements of a successful business plan.

(1) You need an executive summary (one page summarizing the whole plan). You need an industry overview, defining the problem you are solving and an overview of the market.

(2) You need a description of your product or the service. How does it serve as a solution?

(3) You need a competitive analysis. What/who is your competition?

(4) You need a sales and marketing plan.

(5) You need to identify your target customer and proof for your concept.

(6) What is your method of operations?

(7) Who's on your management team, your board of advisers, your dream team?

(8) What are your financial projections?

(9) You need to outline your risk analysis and appendix.

If you are going to raise capital, you don't just talk to an investor. I get people all the time that come to me saying they have an idea, and boom… it's on a napkin. They tell me that they just need $100K for 10 percent. I ask if they can send me their business plan. They then ask me what I mean when I say 'business plan.' If they don't have one, that means I am going to end up giving them 100K and never see it again.

One of the most important parts of raising capital is coming up with a reasonable ask, and then explaining how the proceeds will be used. Many entrepreneurs don't understand this. For example, a guy came on *Shark Tank* saying he needed 150K for 10 percent of his company. I asked what he was going to use the 150K for?

His response was essentially this, "Well, I am going to use the money as a down payment for a piece of real estate where we are going to build a building, then launch the business."

"Okay, so you are going to build the building and then equip the building with furniture. Where is that money going to come from?" I asked. He said once he got the real estate, then they would figure out that batch of money at that time. I told him, "$150K dollars doesn't get you in business. $150K dollars gets you a piece of land. How are you going to build the business, generate revenue, and pay me back?" This guy told me he thought I would have more money for him after that. I said, "Well, no. You are not going to get the first batch of money based on the answers you are giving me."

Instead, he should have said he was going to lease a small office and start generating massive amounts of revenue with the money I gave them. Then, pay me back all of my money, plus a huge return on my investment, and then build it into a global business. That's what I wanted to hear. I want to know that people have a successful business plan, a successful marketing plan, and then I will talk about how to go about raising the capital, how to call on investors, and what the sweet spots are for the investors.

The bottom line on raising capital is, you can't just go build yourself a huge global business without thinking about how you're going to finance it. In the old days, I thought if I built a successful business, money was going to be easy. It's not, unless you know how to do it. There's an art to raising capital. Part of it involves making sure you are prepared and know how to pitch your business properly.

The Perfect Pitch

While the actual product or service you are trying to sell is a critical part of the process, it is just as important to sell the customer on yourself, your services, and your business. Even though I have made thousands upon thousands of pitches, have spoken to thousands of people, and have seen a great amount of success, I still pitch myself and my businesses. No matter who you are, or what you do, you have to be ready to drop the perfect pitch. It doesn't matter if you are going to make this perfect pitch in front of a crowd of thousands, or a crowd of one. To help with the concept of a perfect pitch, I have created a 10-step system.

Before you can start perfecting the perfect pitch, you have to ask yourself a couple of questions. What are you pitching? In other words, what product, business, or service are you trying to sell? Next, what do you want to get out of this pitch? More customers? More sales? Nonetheless, these questions are for you to answer, and you need to answer them before devising your perfect pitch. The perfect pitch can be broken down into these 10 steps:

(1) The **Tease** is your hook; the period of time when you plant the seed. This is when you reveal a problem. You have to explain to your customers why you are giving the pitch. You also have to use showmanship, which sets the pace for the rest of the pitch. If your showmanship skills are demonstrated in the Tease portion of your pitch, then you will have your audience (or your customer) hooked from the very beginning.

(2) Next up is **Please**. In this part of the perfect pitch, you are telling your customer how your product or service can solve the problem you mapped out in the first step. Ideally, your product or service will solve this stated problem in the most efficient, elegant, and cost-effective way. You have to relay to your customer that your solution is the best solution, and it will solve the problem better than anything (or anyone) else. It is important to also show off your features and benefits, and to display the magical transformation that will take place.

(3) The third step to the perfect pitch is **Demonstration/Multi-functionality**. First, you have to ask yourself if you can demonstrate your product, your service and your value. This is the key to any successful pitch, and it brings multi-functionality to the forefront. It shows it off. Think of this step as an added value. Ideally, your service or product is multifunctional. If you can show this off to your customer, then you just brought bonus points to the table.

(4) But Wait There's More! is the fourth step, and it's not just for infomercials on TV. This is the step where you give more value to your product or service by showing and adding more to the pitch—maybe added bonus items or "buy 2 get 1 free if you act now" incentives. At this point, your customer should already be biting, but now is the time to really win them over. So, show them what else you have to offer.

(5) Testimonials are the fifth step to creating the perfect pitch. You are now using someone else to do the pitching. In other words, who says so besides you? This is the proof behind your business, product, or service. Testimonials can include consumers (actual users of the product or service), professionals (leaders in your industry), editorial (articles, experts, press, journals, trade publications, magazines, newspapers), etc. Testimonials can also feature celebrities. Celebrity testimonials can be very powerful for the simple fact that people love celebrities. Then there are documented testimonials, which can include clinical studies, labs tests, and science. Once again, this is one of the most important areas for creating the perfect pitch.

(6) Another important step is **Research and Competitive Analysis**. For this step, you should be asking yourself if you have done your research. If so, then this is the portion of the perfect pitch when you show off all of that information. This can include information on the industry, market and competitors. It can also be facts, figures, and statistics. This research should show off the fact that you, your company, and your product/service is unique.

(7) The seventh step is **Your Team.** In this step, you are bringing the credibility of your team and putting it right there on the metaphorical table. Who makes up your team? It could be advisers, management, directors, and strategic partners. Your team will help scale, open connections, add on the knowledge factor, and so much more.

(8) Why? is the eighth step. Why are you pitching? How will the person in front of you help? This step will change based on who you are actually pitching to. For example, if you are looking for funds, then this is a big section, and you need to incorporate many talking points.

(9) The ninth step is **Marketing Plan.** You have done your pitch and given out all your information. Now, how will you make everything happen? For instance, you need to know your marketing and distribution plan. As is the case throughout your entire pitch, it is essential that you show confidence. Sell whoever you are pitching on your product or service, and yourself as well. People invest in people all the time.

(10) The 10th and final step is **Seize**. You laid everything out, now ask! What are you trying to accomplish? Ask it! Being the final step, this is the time to present the final call to action.

Remember, each pitch will be different. Some pitches last for over an hour and others last only a few seconds or minutes. It just depends on how much time you are given or how much time you need. That is why you need to craft your pitches accordingly. Practice, practice, and more practice.

***

To contact Kevin:

www.KevinHarrington.tv

Joel Sauceda

Joel Sauceda is a self-made entrepreneur who got his start in the direct marketing industry at the age of 19. Known as the "Dot Com Guy", Joel has broken multiple records in the Online marketing & Direct Sales industry and is responsible for multi-million dollars in revenues over the past 20 years.

Joel has launched and sustained numerous Online and off-line ventures in his 21year business career. Joel is Founder of VortexAlliance.com, his personal coaching & mentoring community and serves on the board of SVJMarketing.com and ROYOL Music and is a partner in Cracking the Rich Code with Jim Britt & Kevin Harrington.

Joel's been featured in numerous publications and has had the honor of meeting Prince William and Harry, and a host of famous athletes and celebrities worldwide.

Joel is the father of two talented children (Veronica 22, Joel 19).

Joel is a former Air Force Reservist and Texas Air National Guardsman and his second passion besides Internet marketing and business is supporting causes that benefit wounded warriors and their families. Joel is also an avid cyclist with a passion for health and wellness.

C Minus to "Dot Com" CEO

How I Found and Re-Discovered My Passion in Life.

By Joel Sauceda

"The Re-Birth of a Passion"

Have you ever heard a song, watched a movie, or caught a glimpse of something or someone that sent chills up and down your spine? Now, I'm not talking about the kind of chills you get when you hear cats fighting or receive a bad newsletter in the mail! I'm talking about the "good chills", and this "classification" of chills often arrive with goose bumps; and, if you're lucky, they're the type that forge memories in our mind that we never forget. These good memories change our lives because they remind us of who you are, what we love, and in my case they've served as reminders that anything's possible!

Before I dive in, try to think of the times in your life when you got these "good chills." The times when you were 100% certain that something good was about to happen for you. Maybe you got "inside info" that the person you had a crush on felt the same, you received the letter of acceptance to the university you dreamed of attending, you heard the shout of "B-6" for that definitive BINGO, or perhaps you were searching for the right career and something or someone inspired you enough to set you on the right path?

If you can't think of a time this happened, it's time to re-discover that flame that's still there because these "chills" are not disposable; they are gifts to you and regardless of how challenging times are, by re-discovering your purpose in life these "chills of enthusiasm" are available to everyone who's open to receive them! The great news is they don't discriminate! Age, ethnicity, or even economic level, are not a factor.

These moments have proven more valuable than any stock or 401K plan in my life; and for a good reason, as you will soon discover, as

I share my own cases of the "chills" spanning over 40 years of my life. I look forward to bringing these moments to life for you as I've discovered how to restore and improve the clarity of these memories each year, much like old movies are brought to life with vivid colors and sound.

The "Chills" Of My Life.

Much of my childhood's memories have become a blur as I've grown older. One of my favorite Jimmy Buffet songs, "A Pirate Looks at 40" left the dock a good 5 years ago as I approach the big 5-0. While most memories have converted from video to pictures in my mind, the "chills" remain in vivid color for instant replay on demand. These moments of awareness are as clear today as they were back in 1986, a time of my youth when I began to realize these feelings might bring value to me. I was right. These "instant replays" have brought comfort and awareness in my darkest times.

So welcome to a small chapter of my life, I hope you gain something from my experience. May the "good chills" race up your spine and serve as a reminder that you are indeed special!

Life on the Air Force base.

My story begins on Dyess Air Force base, in Abilene Texas, where my father was stationed as an NCO (non-commissioned officer). It was there, in the fall of 1983, where I experienced my first "Chills of Enthusiasm". No, these chills did not involve a crush on a girl or a BMX bike that I so longed for; but rather, they involved a cheesy 80's movie about young people "conquering" the world with technology (Real Genius).

The rivalry, the drama, and to add to the memory the famed Tears for Fears song "Everybody Wants to Rule the World", played somewhere in the movie. That movie was responsible for many daydreams where I imagined owning one of the powerful computers these kids were hacking on. I was a technology junky early on in life, however the closest thing I had to a computer was a calculator watch that was missing a few buttons. And how can I forget my cherished "Speak & Spell" toy computer which displayed the recommended ages that were clearly below my age group. Adding insult to injury the Texas Instruments calculator my Dad would bring home from his Air Force job each day was off limits, so just dreaming of what I saw in that movie would have to do for a time.

Yes, an 80's movie was a catalyst for the technology field that's been a major part of my life today; and yes again, that movie and THAT song gives me "chills of inspiration" even to this day! Even though I knew absolutely nothing about real computers at the time, do we ever really know anything or everything we become passionate about in life? Curious enthusiasm for the computer led me to believe beyond a shadow of a doubt that I wanted one, and if I could ever get my hands on one I'd never let it go. I got to the point where I would do everything it took to understand and learn how and why they were so powerful.

Texas Instruments to The Rescue Despite Being Crushed by The Apple!

A short time after watching that movie my future was presented to me once again in the form of a refurbished, discontinued Texas Instruments computer that my father brought home one evening. The $50 clearance price tag was a good enough deal for my father to pick it up from the Texas Instruments factory (which also resided in Abilene, Texas) and bring it home.

To this day I don't believe my father knew just how passionate I was about computers and what that "thrifty purchase" would mean to me. Furthermore, I'm not 100% sure this purchase was even meant for me; but, my passion was so strong for this computer that nobody was going to own it but me. It was going to become my new best friend as I dove headfirst into the manual that accompanied this silver alien ship looking computer/keyboard. I marveled at how I could create moving pictures and even make up my own robot on screen that could ask questions and lead someone down a path who followed the blinking prompts that I had learned to create. Even the Archie comics, and the baseball in the back yard that I loved, took a backseat to this antiquated piece of technology. I later found out it was discontinued thanks to Mr. Steve Jobs company called Apple. They put that computer out of business and I was passionately working and learning on technology that was obsolete. That would not stop me, something else would and it wasn't my love for the computer.

Time and Money Separated Me From My Love Of All Things Tech.

Roll forward a couple of years with me if you would. The military soon moved our family to another base in a far off land called San Antonio, Texas. Allow me to set the stage for you once again. We lived in the basic housing that non-officer families were given (the other side of the tracks). Within these walls I grew up with penny pinching parents who were opposed to name-brand anything! If we wanted anything beyond the basics, we had to cut the grass and in return we'd receive a whopping $3. We also got the right to use Dad's lawn mower for my side grass cutting "ventures". As I type this I can still hear my Mom scolding my brother and sister, and yes, me too! Some parents "scolded", my Mom's voice was SCALDING as she would lace her shouts with threats of belts to our butts from our Dad (I just got "bad chills"!). My parents did not believe in hand-outs and prohibited us from even accepting money from our Grand Parents! Grandma would always sneak it to me. Love you Grandma!

Back to my parents.

Mom was strong and wasn't the coddling type. I do not recall one time, as a child or teen, where she said she loved me. Mom grew up on the ranch and saying "I Love You", as I later learned, was a sign of weakness. Feelings of excitement were also frowned upon in our house as well. Saying I'm excited or expressing it was like speaking a different language. I learned to suppress my excitement because my parents lived by the rule of "Never Get Your Hopes Up." This stuck with me for many years; looking back I know this was one of the causes for not allowing myself or others to be happy at many junctures in my life. And do I blame my parents? No. I've learned that every family has their issues and if my parents brought me up the way they were brought up, my life would have been even more challenging. Saying "I Love You" are words we say today. When I've been in the darkest times in my life my Mom and Dad have always been there, even if I was too stubborn to ask for their help. I Love you, Mom and Dad.

My parents provided us with our basic needs and occasionally a few "wants."

Mom was not a "phony" as she likes to say and she was one hell of a multi-tasker! She could discipline, cook, clean, and smack us with a fly swatter when we had it coming! She would also deliver a dinner for the family just in time for my father's usual 5:30 arrival at home. This is where my LIFE listening skills took shape.

Dad would grace the table wearing a t-shirt, along with the other half of his Air Force uniform, and we would all hold hands singing sweet Jesus songs together! LOL (that's laughing out loud for you non-millennial). It was not like this in our home.

Now that I look back on it, these dinners were more like therapy sessions for my pops. Dad would spill his guts to Mom while devouring his dinner. We'd here all about his worries and challenges at work, and I'm not sure if my brother and sister internalized this but I was the ultimate "eavesdropper." Information was great data, good or bad, but in my parents' house we were only allowed to listen and I did just that.

Fortunately for my Dad, Mom was a great listener. A woman of opinions, and after listening, she would air them uncensored! Yes, it was entertaining at times but looking back it was these dinner conversations that I took to heart and I found myself fearing adult money problems. I feared these more than my junior high school report cards. You see, my parents were not the type that micro-managed our schooling. If we had homework it was up to us to do it, and simply passing was more important than getting an "A". So, a "C" was the safety net I strived for because I hated school. I wanted the last 5 years of my schooling sentence to come to an end as soon as possible. Middle school and high school were not great memories for me.

I was embarrassed at the non-name brand shoes I had to wear. The fear of a fellow classmate pointing out something that I was wearing, that his mom donated to the base "Thrift Shop" where my Mom would sometimes find our clothes, was always there. I was always embarrassed and worried about what others would think of me if the tag on my blue jeans was not RED (remember the 501's?). I'd color the orange tag red, or make KMART Non-Nike's into Nike's by using a razor blade to make the square logo into a SWOOSH. Looking back, it was insanity, but in those times I worried about those things. And like father like son, I often worried about not being good enough or losing everything. Today I think about just how much I was like my Dad growing up, yet we rarely compared notes! What a resource we could have been to one another.

These experiences taught me to adapt to any situation, not because I was book smart but because in my mind those things were essential to survival in the school where I was forced to attend.

More Junior & High School Therapy.

Allow me to spend one more paragraph on the school subject.

I didn't dislike school, I HATED it. I thought the home comings and dances and "mums" (who the hell named them that!?) were bullshit. I remember classmates excited for the lunch bell. Why? The food sucked, and worst of all the entire seating "situation" was enough for me to skip lunch as often as I could so I didn't have to guess which lunch table clique I fit in with. And one more thing, my Mom worked outside the cafeteria as a hall monitor, imagine that!

So I was a kid with a MULLET, a few Iron Maiden & Def Leppard t-shirts, bleached out jeans, a dangling grim reaper earring, and knock-off Nike's. Not much piqued my interest in school; well, with the exception of typing class where Mrs. Shultz taught me how to type 60 words per minute. Today I type faster than I speak! (How cool that Mrs. Shultz and I are friends on Facebook today, gotta' love technology!)

I viewed school as a prison sentence and was simply doing my time. I firmly believed that when I got out of school I would find my way and it was NOT going to be college. I would someday be in business for myself. But, that's for another day another chapter.

So what happened, why was I not involved in school? Why was I not on the baseball team and why did I not hang out with the "NERDS"? Why, the computer. The love of my life, the computer, had changed so much from the time of my first contact with that discontinued model. While my father did all he could to provide us with computers, I had forgotten how much I loved them. It would be several years beyond my eventual C MINUS graduation, in which I darted across the stage because I was now free, that we would re-engage.

Beyond High School.

College was something I was not interested in, especially after discovering the cost (Mom & Dad were not footing that bill!). Coming to the realization that the courses I would have to take all had the word PRE before them (Pre-Algebra etc), I was not going to waste any time in the school environment again.

So rolling forward once again, it was 1999 when I caught the tail end of another movie that grabbed my attention. Another movie that featured that "CHILLING" song "Everybody Wants To Rule The World", "Pirates Of Silicon Valley." As I type this I'm grateful to that movie for reuniting me with my passion and a new passion I had discovered between the age 18 and 30, The Direct Sales Industry.

Direct Sales &Technology.

For the past 20 years I've dedicated my life to connecting these two passions. I experienced success in several Direct Sales industries leading up to 1999 when I saw "Pirates Of Silicon Valley". Once again I dove headfirst into discovering how I could marry the two. In 2001 I co-founded a tech-marketing company, and recently co-founded another tech company that makes marketing with technology easier for people from all walks of life and it is worldwide. This passion keeps me awake and motivates me day in and day out to improve and grow within these two life-changing industries. While there is so much more I could share, beyond one chapter, I'll leave that for another time.

For now, I must give thanks to the people I attribute the successes to, and overcoming the many failures that these industries have graciously provided me!

First I want to thank my Dad. A man of strong work ethic, integrity, and a love for his children and grandchildren that goes beyond anything I could ever understand. Next, I want to thank my Mom. She supported her husband through interactions and instilled a toughness in me that I'm so grateful for today.

And who else?

As Jimmy Buffet says in one of his songs, "I've learned from pirates and saints." I'll only thank the "saints" for now. I thank the late Dayle Maloney. I also thank David Manning, James Wiggins, Rick Lentini for teaching me so much and of course, the humble but wise Jim Britt, for the wisdom they've instilled in me to this day.

In closing, I've learned that it does not take a huge village to build a legacy; but rather true friends like Efrain Valdez, Andre Johnson "FNS" who've all contributed to a common vision each and every day. People who put others before their own wants in life and lead with their passion for what they do.

Last but not least, a huge shout out to my two amazing children who will someday carry my legacy on.

Until next time.

***

To contact Joel:

JoelSauceda.Com

CEO/ DOT COM Ventures

CEO/Founder VortexAlliance.Com

Carla Walker

Carla Walker MFT has practiced for over 25 years inspiring individuals, couples and business owners as a Spiritual/Intuitive Coach. She's fortunate to work with high profile celebrities in the music, film and racing industry. She is a co-author Cracking the Rich Code, an expert in the documentary film, "Imagine a World". She is known as, "The Changer."

Many have benefited from her unique and enthusiastic style. Her passion lies in motivational speaking, teaching topics such as mindful living, meditation, how to cook simple plant-based meals, how to direct the mind, and finding/following your golden path. Trained as a Pranayama Meditation level 111 teacher, she runs workshops combining meditation, the Gene Keys and a simple plant-based meal.

As a young girl, Carla was always on a quest. By age 5 she knew she wanted be a teacher. At age ten, she was introduced to the Eastern path of meditation through Self-Realization Fellowship. Her balanced life includes time with her children, grandchildren and friends, experimenting with new Vegan recipes, exercising including Spartan races, and time in nature. As a visionary, Carla knows she is here to assist humans in connecting to their higher consciousness and evolution through the Gene Keys.

The Joyful Rich Human Life

By Carla Walker

Do you know your code to living a rich life? Are you already wealthy? What if you're rich now and missing it? Developing your identity as a happy, rich person is key. Living a prosperous life is knowing what your seeking moves from within out.

I'm excited to be on this journey with you. If you were drawn to read this chapter, trust somewhere somehow, we're aligned. This powerful information will help you SHIFT to a new identity. Your own exceptional self is here to bring something unique to the planet. Your DNA is richly coded just for you.

This chapter includes paying attention to the clues, getting conscious to high-vibing food and people, remembering our energy is a frequency, living a daily practice, and more.

Are you listening to the Clues? If you already have a strong inner guidance system, or clues to your purpose, write them down. If you feel uncertain, this is where contemplation is essential in getting you directly on your path: Clues or Purpose

_____

_____

_____

_____

_Mark Completed ___

A Fun story about a clue. It was a Tuesday at 5:00 PM when a coaching client asked me to give him feedback on a coach named Britt. I said I would get back to him. I closed my office and went to my computer. I was listening because this is not something I would do at this time. Usually, I would go start dinner. I went to my email, and there sat an email from a Jim Britt. At the time, I thought the email was from my client regarding the coaching program he wanted me to review. I texted him and said, "I have the information on Jim." He said the person he was referring to was female. I was perplexed for a moment. I smiled because Jim, whom I never met before, was asking me to write a chapter in this book. Jim and I connected so naturally. It all moved with ease. I'm now writing in this powerful, life changing book. I want you to be in tune with listening and following the clues.

A friend of mine sent her young teenager up to audition for a commercial. She dropped him off and went to find parking. He came down and said, "Mom, I got the cereal commercial."

She said, "No, you were supposed to audition for a different company." She asked him to run back up to a different floor. On that day, he booked two commercials. He was following his inner guidance system. It's always working and available to us. Just take a breath and access it. We forget and start thinking instead of listening.

Achieving a level of **joy through service** is what makes you a million/billionaire. Are you enjoying the variety of experiences life is offering you now, this moment? Many humans are just focused on making millions. The journey to making your millions is not the destination. At the end of your life, when you evaluating your journey, you will most likely ask yourself, *how did I do in my relationships, was I of service to others?*

What is your meaning of wealth? Stop for a moment to contemplate. I have not met or coached a millionaire/billionaire who ever just stopped and thought, *I'm here, I'm rich. I made it.* The mind will want more. It will continue to seek. Making millions is not the end of the story for a person desiring wealth. You'll become dissatisfied if you don't have some type of a spiritual, mental and physical practice.

Just a reminder-You're rich today!

Begin with a deep breath into your belly. Do you know how powerful a deep breath is to staying present? Drop your jaw, shoulders and stories now. Take a breath into the Now.

What is your daily practice and what does this have to do with cracking the rich code? EVERTHING! We have been programmed to focus on money. Money will come when we start living our lives on our uniquely designed path.

We're going to start and finish each day with a few habits that will take only minutes to implement. Do you know the word Kaizen? It's a Japanese word for continuous improvement of working practices.

How do you begin your day and at what time? The top most successful people **rise early**. I wake at 4:05 am. I used to wake at 4:10 and felt rushed. Choosing to adjust just five minutes made my morning run smoothly. This may seem like a silly adjustment, but it's the difference between staying in joy or dropping into a less-than-joyous state. **STOP NOW**. Breathe for a moment and ask yourself, *when is the best time for my highest self to rise up for the day?* Put the time in your calendar and alert your phone to repeat daily. Mark Completed____

MAKE YOUR BED — Simple, yes. But watch your mind tell you why you don't need to do it in the morning. **Do you know you have about 5 seconds before the saboteur shows up and tells you not to worry about making the bed?** Who's going to see it? It's a small, but very important muscle. You want to beat your saboteur! Write and alarm your phone. Mark Completed ____

SMILE MEDITATION – The benefits of mediation are spoken about everywhere, but my experience is that most people don't have a regular practice. Benefits include reduced stress, increased mental focus, decreased anxiety, improved sleep, increased ability to stay in the present moment and love more people.

Either in or out of bed, begin with bringing your awareness into your breath. It's an easier time to focus on the breath due to our minds not yet being stepped into gear. Set a simple intention: 1, 5, 10, or 20 plus minutes? A simple breath into the belly. Notice your belly rising and heart opening. Release the breath fully. Notice the body without any attachment. Put your lips in a smile position. The brain will read the smile movement and begin to register happiness. The brain is connected to our body's response. When taking this action with my lips, any time of day, it makes me laugh. This action raises my magnetic frequency.

If you feel more comfortable, download an application for guided meditation. The important thing is to do it now. If you can be consistent with one minute, stay with one minute until it's a habit no matter what is happening in your life. After your breath work, ask in your mind's eye for any information and guidance to activate or understand your higher purpose. Alert your phone now and hit repeat. Mark Completed _____

CONTEMPLATION- Many cultures take time to **sit**. Think back. In the last week, when did you stop just to listen and be? Look at your calendar now. Where is there space? Take your phone and block out a time. This is a gift to yourself. Do you want to set the goal for 30 minutes? Cell phone off. Mark Completed _____

CONCENTATION- Spiritual Guru, Paramahansa Yogananda, taught the importance of concentration. A daily practice is powerful. Implement a simple affirmation – "I'm enjoying living richly, on purpose, contributing daily to myself and the planet" at the end of your meditation. Learning to discipline the mind, along with maintaining a joyful frequency, is most vital for creating/manifesting thought into matter.

Mindful daily habits build identity and increase your magnetic field. As you up your mood from lethargy, despair or anger (lower frequency feelings) your magnetic field aligns with your true heart's desire.

Why do we care about our frequency/Megahertz? When you focus the mind on being in the higher tones (such as love, peace, and joy) we begin to design and align with creating matter. Natural ideas, solutions, and human support appears. Keeping your body radiant, increases your chances for living a more fully integrated life.

There are ways to measure a frequency/vibration. In music, each note has a vibration. We're simply particles of light with a vibrating a tone. Just stay open to this concept. Healers are living music, helping us shift to the higher vibration/notes. They're measuring emotions and how the sound of a note changes our moods. Illness does not live in the higher notes. Fear, guilt, sadness, anger, love, peace, joy, bliss. it's all measurable.

Each habit will either raise or lower your tone. This contributes to attracting/living your true purpose. Positive habits pull it all into alignment, cracking the code. We're all designed to be radiant, happy, successful beings.

LISTENING– How well do you listen? How do you know what you're listening too?

I started a seasonal, gourmet coffee business called Peppermint Farms with my former husband back in 1987. He asked how I knew about the coffee? I said I could see and feel it was going to be big. It just felt right in my belly. I would feel energized when I spoke about it. It led to opening a coffee house café on the coast. **If your body is not giving you a clear YES, the answer is NO**. The more you listen to belly/solar plexus responses, the clearer you'll understand it. A great question to ask yourself is, *am I thinking or feeling?*

Building on simple habits, a simple agreement with yourself is to heat water and add a lemon slice. It has immense health benefits – immune boosting, helps with digestion, increases metabolic rate, detoxifying, Ph balancing, hydrating, helps you poop, anti-inflammatory, etc. This habit may take one more minute of your day, but it's well worth it. It's a wonderful ritual of nurturing oneself. Alert phone calendar now. Mark Completed ____

A **cold shower**- When showering, turn the handle to cold. Focus on your breathing. It's okay to scream. This practice may lower blood pressure, stimulate weight loss, speed up muscle recovery and relieve depressive symptoms. It's such a wake-me-up habit! It always makes me smile.

How's your quality of life? Don't wait to start a self-care practice. These teachings are simple yet life changing in contributing to good health. Can you feel yourself reaching spiritual, mental and physical equilibrium?

Do you feel vibrant? The goal is to resonate over 700 Megahertz, the measurement for joy. This frequency is a massive clue for cracking the code. This is manifesting is at its best.

SHIFTING - Check in now. What do you think your energy is resonating? If you feel dense, STOP now and put your hands in the air. If physically safe, begin to jump up and down. Continue for one minute. How's your energy level? Did it increase? Did it make you smile?

Do you know there is an evolution happening and it's the food industry? A client of mine just got it! He said, "I can feel the difference when I don't eat the right food." There is a vibration to food. If you eat fast food, most likely, there is not a lot of nutritional value to give you energy and magnetism. At first you may feel the carbohydrate high, but stop and check in with your body. Do you feel more joy after you eat that type of food?

It can be measured that highly processed foods, GMO, foods with chemical additives, meat, poultry, microwaved, over cooked foods, fruits and vegetables picked early leave you feeling dull, foggy, perhaps depressed, and lacking your natural energy. If you choose high-vibing food and stay in gratitude while eating, you'll feel an increase in your magnetism.

Our consciousness is shifting and we're beginning to choose higher quality foods. Stay conscious, and at the end of the day ask yourself, *did I feed my body live foods?*

Do you take **Supplements**? I'm not a nutritionist or doctor of medicine so please check with your doctor before starting any supplements or dramatically change your diet. I wish we could get all our nutrients from eating clean foods. I tried and will continue to eat clean, but due to improper farming of our soil, it's deficient from minerals, vitamins and microbes and therefore unable to feed our bodies. If you diet or eat highly processed foods, you may be malnourished. It's not just about eating organic. Organic is best, but may still be lacking in the necessary vitamins and minerals.

Over the years, I have found clients come in and say they're depressed. They're usually deficient in B complex, Vitamin D, and Magnesium. Have your doctor run a blood panel. Low D is connected to low moods. B's are my natural energy supplements. Many female clients are low in Progesterone. Our hormones affect our moods. Most humans today are low in Magnesium due to filtered water and our diets. Magnesium has so many benefits such as helping us get a good night sleep.

Consider the possibility you may need supplements. I follow a plant-based life style and see the world is evolving. Many of you are waking up and feel uncomfortable eating animals or want to change the earth's blue print. I used to think my sluggishness was due to not having enough animal protein. Plants have plenty of protein. I don't believe you know people sick from lack of protein? It was honestly live plant- based food and supplements. I have consistent energy throughout the whole day and feel amazing.

If you're suffering or muscling through life, **find a good Integrative Doctor**. Why would you continue to walk around feeling lethargic, moody, struggling to get off the couch and/or yelling out of control. Fix it and call today. Mark Completed

---

Do people describe you as joyful?

Remember – getting on track with your life code is going to elevate you and the planet.

NO NEWS-Any chance you're willing to give it up for one week? I highly recommend it. Many clients have asked, "How will I know what's going on in the world?" The information you need will come to you. If you want to know the weather, ask Siri. Skip the drama. Believe it or not, this world is becoming a better planet. The news scares humans and may contribute to you living in a lower vibrational state. If you pay attention, when you get together with your friends or colleagues, you'll find yourself retelling the same scary stories about the tragedies on the planet. Remember, we're shooting for you to vibrate at 700 hertz. Is hearing or retelling chilling news stories contributing to your elevation to a joyful state? Do you want your mind creating scary or inspired thoughts and feelings?

ARE YOU WILLING TO GIVE UP NEGATIVE STORY TELLING? – What inspired me to stop telling myself and others so many stories were the beginning of understanding just what I was activating. The process of our thinking and feeling creates my heaven or brings awareness to my pain/body. Each story vibrates and creates in the lower or higher realms. There is a vibration to all words/sounds. Decide for one week to watch your story telling. Our minds may resist and your story telling may begin, but practice thought stopping. Daily phone reminder. Mark Completed _____

ARE YOU WILL TO TELL FUN, INSPIRING, FUTURE DREAM STORIES? Choose a few of your favorite high-vibing friends and be sure you have fun sharing your awesome dream stories. Don't hold back or minimize. Embellish and let yourself feel amazing. There is no dream too big. Do you remember how to play? Daily phone reminder set. Mark Completed _____

FORGIVING- Stop reading now and make a list of 5 people you're willing to forgive. It may be a family member, boss, neighbor, partner, past friend, yourself, etc. Decide now to consciously forgive them. Promise yourself you'll stop the storytelling.

Write down: I forgive ____(Name)_____ for _____(story)_____ and I love ___(Name)_____. Say it a few times until you feel neutral. It will continue to move the energy out of your body. Practice this on a regular basis. It works. If you do it and your body is in strong disagreement, it will soften and shift to the love frequency shortly. Mark Completed_____

BEING/LIVING IN SERVICE- We're moving from being self-focused to a collective consciousness. After we learn about self-love, the next evolutionary state is giving back to experience our greatest joy. Being in service is a clue to cracking your rich code. It's one of the fastest ways to raise our feelings.

Where are you currently giving back? What inspires you? Contemplate how well you did in the last week giving to your relationships? Do you have a neighbor who's isolated? Can you share a meal with a neighbor? Call a friend instead of text. People need to hear the tone of your voice. They will feel your love. Picking up the phone and donating to a charity is still a feel-good act.

Remember if we're all rich, then we have plenty of energy to give somewhere. By chance, did your story teller show up and tell you why you can't give because you're too broke, tired or busy? It's a funny story that will keep you from being radiantly rich.

I hope this has helped you crack your rich code.

I wish you all love, peace, joy, success, good health and may you allow your dreams to come into reality.

A portion of the proceeds will be donated to Charity Water.

***

To Contact Carla:

Telephone 1-661-803-1352

www.carlascounseling.com

Facebook   - https://www.facebook.com/CarlaWalkerLifeCoach/notifications/

Instagram -https://www.instagram.com/carlajean45/

SKYPE- carlajean45

Linked -https://www.linkedin.com/in/carla-walker-08879b10/

Norman Charles Dupas

Norman Charles Dupas is a seasoned business professional with 30 years of diversified leadership experience as a business owner, marketing/business consultant, and award-winning pharmaceutical sales representative.

As a visionary executive, Norm conceptualizes unique business, sales, and marketing concepts to provide a competitive edge and capitalize on market niches. With a consistent track record of analyzing and re-engineering organizations of varied sizes in different sectors, he has successfully improved companies' revenues, efficiencies, corporate image, customer service, employee culture, and bottom line profits. With a financial acumen, he can develop measurable metrics for performance and analyze financial data to identify targeted strategic business and financing plans.

As a founder, entrepreneur and senior leader of several businesses (Niva 10 Corp., Thermea Nature Spa by le Nordik in Winnipeg, Cottages at Clear Lake, CinDen Nutritionals, and Labelle Florists), he has a proven track record of recognizing opportunities and bringing individuals and groups together for a common cause to form successful enterprises.

Acknowledged for his enthusiasm, sense of humour and motivational personality, Norm can build consensus with and inspire team members to meet organizational objectives and high standards. Norm is fully bilingual in English and French.

How to Bring Your Business And Your Life To Level 10!!!

By Norman Charles Dupas

Many incredible people have had an influence on my life, but it is my father and mother who have had the greatest impact, and it is to them that I dedicate this chapter. My father was my mentor and hero, while to this day my mother continues to show me how to live life full of passion, laughter and to youthful exuberance. My parents taught me to respect people regardless of who they are, what they do, where they live or what they believe. Most importantly my parents taught me to respect myself and to do what I love. *"Success is not the key to happiness. Happiness is the key to success. If you love what you are doing, you will be successful"*. Albert Schweitzer.

I have been on a quest to live my life on and with a purpose, measurably at level 10. My intent is to always 'show up' and in doing so, make a difference in peoples' lives. One of the most influential managers I ever worked with told me that 90% of life is just showing up. In other words, if you are not happy with a situation, then do something about it, and make the necessary changes to improve the situation.

I am often asked what living life at a level 10 means? To me it means that in everything you do you bring your passion and you're A game. When you are vibrating at a level 10 you can feel it in the core of your soul. Everything taste better, everything sounds better the colours are brighter. Conversations flow like your swimming downstream, effortlessly. Time seems to stand still but passes by like a flash of light.

I named my company nivå10 which is Swedish for Level 10. I was pleasantly surprised when I discovered that Jim Britt had developed a program – "Live Life @ Level 10". The power to live life at a level 10 is in your hands.

I asked Jim what living life at a level 10 means to him.

Living Life @ Level 10 is about developing the understanding of how simple life can be when you decide to reinvent yourself and open yourself up to a new way at looking at and handling everyday conflicts.

You can't force anything into existence. You can't make a miracle happen. You can't make someone else do certain things to fit into your way of thinking. The only person you are in control of is you.

Most are so focused on their problems that they are blinded to new solutions. Their imagination is working overtime focused on all the things that are wrong in their life.

For example: a person wants to be happy and yet they focus on all the things that make them unhappy. Another wants to have more money, yet they focus on all the reasons they are broke

More than ever, people are being called to stop living superficially, to let go of a life of "should do's," and to create authentic purpose-driven days full of happiness, success and wealth. That's what living Life @ Level 10 is all about.

And why is it that if that's what everyone wants, why don't they make the changes to live that way?

First off...the reason why our learning efficiency and ability to make changes falls so quickly is because the brain needs time to process what it has learned. By piling on too much information at one time, the brain's <u>working memory</u> cannot effectively process everything, so it discards most of it.

The level 10 program is a systematic approach to making radical improvements in your life, with small bite sized input. Because, the way we learn and develop new habit patterns is to revisit similar uplifting messages with a time lapse in between each message. This will move the information from short-term memory to long-term memory, and then to application.

In the case of personal development, you hear a message once, but often times your old programs and beliefs contradict, take over and discards the message. If you want to master a concept, the best method is training the mind to listen and create a new paradigm through repeated input of empowering messages.

*Learning and mastering any principle is also a **self-reinforcing process**. Which means that learning one thing can boost mastering another. For example, when you overcome a fear, with that you'll naturally develop more confidence... a double win!*

*When it comes to **learning**, the more ways you approach your mind with an empowering message, the better it'll be stored as a new subconscious program, and the better it can later be remembered and utilized.*

We are all naturally successful, happy individuals whether we realize it or not. But, the reality is that most spend about 90% of their time and energy dealing with non-productive feelings and emotions and focused on what they don't want. We literally become addicted to unconscious behaviors and beliefs locked away in our subconscious programs that actively block our ability to tap into our true potential and experience the life we deserve.

The power of the mind, in particular the subconscious mind, is unlimited yet can be elusive and restrictive if not managed properly. But, when you start to apply what you've learned it further deepens the retention process.

The level 10 lessons and messages are designed to unlock the power of your mind and create impactful and long lasting change. It is designed to reprogram your subconscious for greater, more rapid success in all areas of your life.

For me, I want participants to receive answers for making their career more successful, their relationships more fulfilling, their family life more harmonious, their financial status more abundant, and much more!

Participants absolutely love this program… and most of all, they love the results they gain from it!

That's what Living Life @ Level 10 is all about."

Take inventory of everything you have right now: your physical, emotional, mental and spiritual health, your drive to educate yourself, the people that you surround yourself with, your material possessions, and your physical condition. These were all obtained by decisions that have shaped your life. The beauty of 'showing up' is that if you are not satisfied with something it allows you to take a new direction – take action, be bold and change the course of your life.

Earl Nightingale proposed that *"we become what we think about".* It is my belief that the same can be said for a business. These thoughts manifest in many ways, ie: a person with a distinct personality, friends and enemies you have, and your team guiding your business in the right direction. The three common faux pas businesses make are parallel to the faux pas people make in their day to day lives. In business, just as in life, problems are ignored and tolerated until they reach a crisis level - the bank loan is called, cash flow is compromised, or a major health challenge arises. The logical approach would be to purpose to prevent these potential catastrophic events from happening. Planning for change before the change affects your plan.

In 1984 my father gave me a fantastic book "In Search of Excellence" by Thomas J. Peters and Robert H. Waterman Jr. Many of the principles in the book continue to hold true today and are what got me started on my own quest to search for excellence, and create the life that I wanted. Ensuring business success can be very simple yet we tend to complicate things. In business, the bottom line is dedicated employees and satisfied customers. Without them, your business will not succeed. It sounds too easy, but the simplest solutions are the most effective. When you focus your attention on people, building and cultivating relationships, your possibilities of success are increased, both in life and in business.

My intention in writing this is to get people excited about their lives and businesses, and to take action in order to live life at a level 10. It is my firm belief that many people are not doing enough to move their life and business forward, and look to complicated concepts to solve their issues of growth. If you are not making positive changes to rectify the challenges in your life and business, a reverse in growth will be experienced, while others who do, are progressing forward!

FAUX PAS # 1: NOT ADMITTING THERE IS A PROBLEM

The first step in evaluating the success of your business is to assess successes and losses, admit there may be a problem, and make plans to correct those issues. Looking over the aspects of your business that need improvement can be overwhelming, maybe even discouraging, but do not despair, there is a light at the end of the tunnel.

The first task is to identify your business' assets and liabilities. If you do not have a clear understanding of what those areas entail, then one of the most efficient methods is to do a survey involving both your customers and employees, who will provide the necessary and valuable feedback. Populating a simple chart that lists the assets and liabilities, will provide a snapshot, an inventory, of where the business is at in that moment in time.

Whereas the 'Why' is important to a company and individual's purpose, the 'What you'd like to achieve' is another vital piece to the success puzzle. How you got there is not as important, and the future or the dream is the most important thing. It is all about the 'what', if you do not know what you want, there is probably a good chance you will never get it.

Understanding where you are at the moment is critical. Admitting that there are challenges and or problems, and putting together decisive plans to tackle them, important and crucial steps towards achieving success in business and living a level 10 life.

FAUX PAS #2: NOT HAVING A ROAD MAP

Once you have identified the obstacles that are in your way on the path to success, you must have a roadmap, a plan on how to deal with them. It is similar to planning a long trip with your family. Without a map it may be difficult to reach your destination. You will eventually find your way but with a little bit of planning you can avoid countless hours of driving around pointlessly.

The business roadmap is a critical element to success. With your team take time to plan your path to success. Knowing what you want and where you want to go are the most important factors in achieving business heights and living a life of happiness and success. When we have clear goals and intentions and we apply focus to them, with perseverance and determination, nothing can sway us from that path to success and happiness. Write down your roadmap and review it often. Your roadmap should be clear enough to see a ten-year target. From there, move to the three-year picture. Next, look at the one-year plan and break this down into ninety day intervals. One thing is for sure, if you know what you want, you will get it. Once you have identified where you are going the next step is to figure out the 'How' to get there.

FAUX PAS #3: NOT GETTING THE PROPER GUIDANCE

When you have identified your assets and liabilities and created a roadmap for change, it is time to take action, and start getting things done. Understanding where your business or life is at and where you want it to go is relatively easy. How to get there takes more time and understanding. It is important to understand that every business and person is different and unique. The definition of wealth and happiness differs in every situation, and understanding these differences is crucial to paving your road to success.

It's critical for your and your company's success to obtain the proper guidance, remember that the best athletes all have coaches. Determine what your needs are and seek out a great "coach" that can bring you to the next level.

Additionally, it is important to remember there is no need to reinvent the wheel. Some basic research of other companies will uncover examples of success and innovation that can be followed step by step. Look for simple solutions, ones that work for you and your business. Success leaves clues.

A checklist can be used regularly to keep you on the right track:

1. Listen to a variety of motivational speakers every day. Each one can inspire you and remind you of the importance of staying focused on the important things. People often say they want to be more positive but are constantly filling their brain with junk. It is virtually impossible to become positive without changing behavior. Albert Einstein's familiar definition of insanity; "doing the same thing over and over again expecting different results" implies that we need to change behaviour in order to see different results.

2. What is consumed and planted in our minds is critical to a level 10 life. If you want to change anything you must have a burning desire to do so. Start telling yourself a story of empowerment and stop any flow of negativity. What you focus on expands. Dream big, imagining how it would look if your life was perfect in every way.

3. Do what you love, this gives you natural energy and provides internal motivation.

4. Commit to excellent, get into the top 10% in your field or industry.

5. Develop a clear sense of direction.

6. Refuse to consider the possibility of failure. If you do not have a way to go back, you must move forward.

7. Invest in your brain and dedicate yourself to lifelong learning. Commit to listening to a podcast or reading a new book weekly. This will continue to fuel the fire. Keep the fires going, your mind focused, and nothing will stop you from achieving your success.

8. *"When the fire dies down, the predators come in!"* (Mike Lipkin) This is from a story about a group of people on an African safari where the keeper tells them that they must continue to put wood on the fire at night otherwise the "predators" will come. In business and life, the predators are the bad thoughts and habits that keep us from moving forward towards our goals.

9. Attitude is everything, be positive. Your life is exactly what you make it through your mental attitude.

10. A popular formula used by a number of successful executives is $E + R = O$. We cannot always control the events (E) that happen to us however we can control the Response (R). By focusing on the Response, we can literally control all Outcomes (O)!

Who do you invest your time with? Surround yourself with the right people. Many years ago, one of my best friends passed away. He was such an amazing person and one of the most positive people I have ever known. A couple of years after he had passed, I found an e-mail from him. The letter attached to this e-mail changed my life. The letter reappeared almost a decade later when a colleague sent it to me once again. Attached to the e-mail was this letter:

Imagine that you had won the following prize in a contest:

Each morning your bank would deposit $86,400 in your private bank account for your own use. However, this prize has rules, just as any game has certain rules…

The first set of rules would be:

Everything that you didn't spend during each day would be taken away from you.

You may not simply transfer money into some other account. You may only spend it.

Each morning upon awakening, the bank opens your account with another $86,400 for that day.

The second set of rules:

The bank can end the game without warning: at any time it can say, "It's over, the game is over!"

It can close the account in an instant and you will not receive a new one.

What would you personally do? You would buy anything and everything you wanted, right? Not only for yourself but for all the people in your life, right? Maybe even for people you don't know, because you couldn't possibly spend it all on yourself and the people in your life, right? You would try to spend every single cent, and use it all up every day, right?

Actually, this game is a reality, but not with money!

Each of us is in possession of such a bank. We just don't see it.

The BANK is TIME!

Each morning we awaken and receive 86,400 seconds as a gift of life, and when the day is done, any remaining time is gone and not credited to us. What we haven't lived up to that day is lost forever.

Yesterday is forever gone…

Each morning the account is refilled, but the magical bank can dissolve our account at any time…WITHOUT WARNING.

So, what will YOU do with your 86,400 seconds? Think about that, and always think of this: Enjoy every second of your life, because time races by so much quicker than we think.

Take good care of yourself, and enjoy life.

Live each day to the fullest, be kind to one another, and be forgiving.

Harbour a positive attitude and always be the first to smile.

Every day is a great day some are just greater than others.

We are all here for a purpose, each of us is unique. Continue your quest to live life at a level 10 and reap all that you sow.

My dream is that everyone takes the opportunity to live life at a level 10.

Life is a gift and can be such a wonderful journey. Design yours now!

***

To contact Norm:

www.normdupas.com

www.livelifeatlevelten.com

Beth Robins

Beth Robins is an evolutionary work in progress, just like you! She has been in the fitness and healthy lifestyle coaching business since 1986. Her lifestyle coaching connects health with wealth encouraging both budding entrepreneurs and people looking to upgrade their health status to step out of their comfort zones and try success on for size!

Beth is a certified personal and group fitness coach who has gathered hundreds of certifications from advanced nutrition principles with Precision Nutrition to the latest trends in fitness as the industry evolves with ACE and IDEA. However, her self-proclaimed PhD in "Been there Done That" continues to serve her in times of crisis, indecision, and epic fails. She has always had the good fortune to run her own businesses as a personal trainer, nutritional consultant, life coach, and entrepreneur. All of this has crafted an incredibly fulfilling career truly helping people step out of their box, take leaps of faith, try new things, discover their raw potential at all stages of life, and finally step into their light!

My goal from this day forward is to stimulate some enthusiasm for your OWN extraordinary journey around the sun!

Starting Over or Just Getting Started?

By Beth Robins

"Cracking the Rich Code"... Well let's start by defining "RICH" for you!

Is it wealth in the stock market, cash in the bank, real estate holdings, mansions, or cars?

OR do you consider more intangible notions to define rich?

Is it great health, a fit body, or a clear, positive, and curious mindset?

Is it having fulfilling relationships and a close family unit?

Is it having a career that makes you look forward to Monday mornings?

OR... Can you possibly dare to have it ALL??? Is there a secret to cracking this code?

It is not a secret! It is intrinsic, but we are blurred by so many distractions that clutter our intuition to see with vision. Most only see obstacles and settle for the path of least resistance and road most taken. We follow the carved route of our ancestors, forgetting that we are the evolved version! Then, a few decades into adulthood some look back and wonder if this is really all there is to life? Is there something missing? There are those who soared early in life and perhaps gained notoriety or fame that was short lived. Our AMAZING veterans returning home from tours of duty enter into civilian life armed with valuable skill sets, but no compass to show them where to go. It can be extremely unsettling, confusing, and unfulfilling, not to mention terrifying! This is not all there is to this gift of life! Now is the time to learn to enjoy mind-blowing experiences, soul stirring stories, and GREATNESS!!!

The most exciting part is that once you learn to see through roadblocks, adapt to change, and actually put action steps to your dreams and goals, ALL of the riches begin to manifest.

You can have abundant wealth and be happy when your vision is aligned. No matter what failures, mistakes, crises, bad luck, or disappointments may come along the way, your core will be solid, and your resolute to keep going will put your path in focus. AND, the most amazing opportunities you never dreamed of will literally land in your lap. This isn't coincidental! It comes when you're ready and able to recognize that the timing is perfect. How do I know??? I know because it's happening to me right now, and I want YOU to be a part of it!

In my early adult years starting out, I always had this nagging voice in my head that I was meant to teach, inspire, entertain, enlighten, and lead people. Great! The problem was I didn't exactly know where I was going with this, or whom I was leading and teaching, and for heaven's sake, where are we going???! I used to be in the entertainment industry as a musical theatre actress. So, at the time, I secretly hoped I'd hit the big time, but my timing was off. It was incredibly fulfilling at the time, but it wasn't sustainable for my next chapter in life. Here I starred as a wife, mother, and consummate "giver". It became impractical to live the life of a late night singing theatre bum while maintaining my role as Super Mom in the wee hours of the morning. So, my singing audience fell to the ears of little ones craving lullabies. Thankfully I had started a "side hustle", if you will, as both a healthy lifestyle coach and a network marketer. These were perfect Mom jobs for me! I could teach, lead, somewhat entertain, get in my own workout time, AND build a very solid residual income for myself for years to come! WIN WIN!!!

Fast-forward 30 years and its time I take a brief look in the rearview mirror. This is an important exercise as it reflects the path that led you to this moment, but isn't necessarily the path of your future self. For me, life wasn't perfect, but it was satisfying and enriching in all the right places. I had a happy quarter of a century marriage and two beautiful children that grew into fierce warriors in their own light. Success! However, I also needed to face a very real transition to divorce, children leaving the proverbial nest, a move to the city from the quiet, yet far too small suburb, and basically an entire life overhaul that some would refer to as "starting over". Guess what? That nagging voice was still chirping away! This time, however, it was a bit louder and more emphatic that I needed to re-identify with who I was as a single woman who had entertained both success and failure, had a thriving personal training business, a circle of friends, old and new, and a brand new chapter waiting to be filled. I needed to hone in on what this voice was trying to say. This "voice" by the way, sings the song of our soul. We all have one, but many times we turn down the volume to follow someone else's voice. I became very in tune with my spirituality and the gentle kicks in the behind from powers greater than me. I realized that there really was no such thing as coincidence and if I just stayed out of my own way, I might experience exponential growth and an extraordinary journey!

This is when the REAL work began! I hired a counselor, sought out my fitness mentor, and began to identify favorite "self-help" gurus that aligned with my sense of humor. I subscribed to a gazillion seminars, webinars, podcasts, and long walks on the lakefront to sort through the clutter, get clear about where I wanted to go, and let the answers unfold. As I came out the other side of this experience, I was armed with a new set of tools, a clear notion of what I wanted out of life, and most importantly W H Y! I am now laser focused on leading my tribe of workout warriors, connecting strategic partnerships, and helping people looking for their own re-purposed reasons for their seasons! The difference here is that I'm compelled to do it in a grander way! The exciting part is that once I began buzzing at a higher frequency, opportunities began to literally fall from the sky! My little dreams of riches and success that used to sit on the shelf whimpering for attention are now forced into the big bad world and I couldn't be more excited! I want to save people the time, trouble, and torment of trying to venture alone. Wouldn't it be amazing if we could figure out not only where we're going, but WHY and HOW at the early stages rather than bumbling along in the status quo? Wouldn't it be a relief to discover your potential roadblocks before wasting time and money? AND how awesome is the idea that just maybe you'll figure out why you haven't succeeded in your quest for a healthier body!

As I indicated, I too have stumbled over obstacles, spent time in the fetal position wishing someone would fix it, felt helpless, anxious, and even lost at times. The fantastic news is this... I not only survived, I learned and grew into the ferociously determined woman I am today!

Whether you're just getting started in life or beginning a new chapter, the process is the same, yet always evolving as you grow into your new, incomparable self! The first step before you proceed is nailing down the fundamentals of just exactly what makes you tick. The secret to ALL successes, be it health, love, or business, is your uniqueness. This is your gift that you are required to share with the world! This is what separates you from the rest and gives you validation that you DO deserve to be rich, happy, and in love. It is your calling card, and it cannot be duplicated by your competition because only YOU know it. However, it is worthless if you don't understand it, harness the power, and use it to your advantage! We start by peeling away the layers so that you can become very clear about your gift!

I have a series of ten questions that will hopefully allow you to dig deep to discover some key elements that might bring light to your journey. It is very important that you check your ego and let go of judgment from here on. There are NO wrong answers, and know that they too could evolve and change as you progress! They are simply YOUR answers.

Don't over think through the process. Just read, absorb, think, and let it unfold! Remember, this exercise is to uncover your OWN Rich Code! The goal is to discover the right path for YOU to be rich in health, relationships, your bank account, and most of all, in life!

What is your WHY???

This is the single most important principle you must define in order to stay focused on your path. This is a very unique and personal part of your story. Obviously we choose a career to earn a living, and choose a healthier lifestyle to improve quality of life, but there has to be more to it or it becomes expendable and arbitrary. So again, ask yourself WHY? Is it to make a difference? To affect change in your world? To insure a longer, higher quality lifestyle? To provide stability for your family? To teach or inspire? To satisfy a curiosity? To please a family member? To climb a ladder? To gain control? To retire early in order to travel, mentor, or volunteer? Define your WHY!

Are your core values aligned with your career goals?

Essentially if this duo is out of whack, you will struggle establishing, and more importantly maintaining a work/life balance going forward. What does this mean?

Your core values are what ground you, validate your decisions, and define your character. They develop early in life. They are unique and might very well diverge from family expectations, which can also cause conflict. It is vital that you listen to YOUR voice here in order to create harmony for yourself. My core values haven't changed. Number one has always been family first. Helping others is second, however there's a new addition on the list...ME! I now make decisions based on taking care of myself physically, emotionally, and professionally. Knowing this, I will not entertain a career offer that would jeopardize my health and well-being. Putting myself in an unhealthy environment including careers that cause undo stress, sleep deprivation, and slim opportunities to eat well, as well as toxic co-workers or clients that drain my energy is no longer an option. This is destined for a very quick burnout! Your career aspirations flow in different stages of life and are circumstantial. Make sure you are not clinging to someone else's notion of who you should be! What is YOUR story?

What gives you joy?

Do you prefer to be in business for and by yourself, or do you enjoy working with a team? Think about what activities, hobbies, causes, and experiences you gravitate toward! This might seem trivial from a business standpoint, so here's a personal example. I have ALWAYS gravitated toward servant leadership in the health coaching realm, but my recent experiences working with various veteran's groups and professional athletes has kept me focused on aligning these into my own next chapter. Add to this recipe circumstances that led me to the wonderful world of CBD (Cannabidiols) BOOM!!! My next chapter is now in full gear networking with top tier connections to bring abundant health, healing, and education to the world! Those "lofty dreams" are now my reality day to day!

Who inspires you?

What books are you reading? Do you listen to podcasts? Are the authors relating to you on a different level? Is there a possibility that you could rub elbows and absorb mentoring from them? Do they have a mastermind group that you could join? Could you be accountable to them? What is it about them that drive you to follow a similar path? Look around you. Who do you spend the most time with? Are you in the presence of thoroughbreds or donkeys? Do they lift you up and hold you accountable? Are they striving for excellence in their own lives? As they say in youth sports, "play up"! Elevate your game and play at the elite level!

What do you NEED to know?

Most often people over think this part. It's a perfect procrastination tool! Obviously if you've decided to proceed into a career that requires more skill, degrees, or training, you'll need to consider that. However, if you're wasting time talking yourself out of it because you are overwhelmed and assume you aren't qualified, then you need to take a step back and sort out why. If you are truly passionate about the possibilities associated with that career direction, then honestly nothing could stop you! You will seek out what you need to know because you have decided to succeed. A solid decision to do something invokes action, while wishful thinking does not!

What is your biggest fear?

This might sound crazy, but many people are afraid of success itself! They are cautious about growing too big and falling hard. I suspect the biggest fear of all is CHANGE! Think about it! Change is inevitable and transcends race, gender, religion, and nationality. We seem to purr when life is copasetic and coasting. When faced with change we withdraw, procrastinate, and resist. It's easier not to do something than to step away from all that is comfortable. Unfortunately, it is one of the only constants in our existence, yet we go out of our way to avoid it! The BIG FOUR on the fear radar are aging, being alone, the unknown, and of course, failure. I truly believe that once you embrace the unknown, take calculated risks, fall and get back up again, and take time alone to reconnect with your own super powers, you eliminate the obstacles because you no longer see them!

If failure is NOT an option, what are your crazy fun dreams?

Have you ever dared to really dream about something you've always wanted to try? If you had a "crazy" idea for a business and everyone thought it was risky and impossible, but you knew deep down it would succeed, would you listen to your critics or follow your dream? Why do we pre judge our own success or assume other's will scoff? We are taught to stay in the box of conformity. Wouldn't it be refreshing to have the mindset that looks far beyond that! Failure is just a sign that you were on the wrong track. It does NOT mean that you are a failure! It's just a step in your learning curve. Thick skin is earned, but if you truly believe in what you are doing and can cast that fear aside, success is imminent.

What do you struggle with in your life?

When it comes to both healthy lifestyle habits and business decisions, I think FOMO comes to mind first. The fear of missing out is such a gut check! Social distractions can derail your healthier path if you don't keep life in balance and in perspective. Some struggle balancing time with family and friends while building a career. Some are serial procrastinators and/or lack organizational skills. There is often the very real struggle with self-doubt and feeling worthy of success. Again, as both a fitness and entrepreneurial mindset coach, know this with all certainty! You deserve a long, healthy and wealthy life!!! Stop tripping over excuses and start your action plan today!

What grounds you?

Tune in to your connection with something bigger than yourself, like religion, nature, spirituality, or for me, the Universal Consciousness. Whatever it is, it keeps you grounded and humble, but more importantly it provides for you! Pay attention to "coincidences!" Prayer, meditation, or simply the power of positive thoughts and intention can often make difficult decisions crystal clear. You will manifest

your thoughts! Negative or positive, it is your focused mindset that will either keep your wheels spinning or let you begin taking advantage of opportunities.

What three new healthy lifestyle choices can you start TODAY?

Pick your top three that you are 99% certain you can master over the next 30 days! Here's a short list to trigger your imagination: flossing more regularly, drinking 70 ounces of water a day, reducing or eliminating alcohol consumption, mindful eating, restorative sleep, intermittent fasting, less sitting, trying something new, regular massage, reading more books, moving/exercising 5 days a week, planning a trip, starting a gratitude journal, seeing a play, shutting down blue screens an hour before bedtime.

Make your own list and COMMIT!!!

Hopefully you're getting closer to understanding who and where you are TODAY realizing you have so much more to offer! You were born with certain gifts and it is your responsibility to share them with the world. If you are in business as an executive or sole proprietor, leading a team or selling a product, remember that your clients and team are buying YOU! They aren't buying your product, course, or seminar. They are buying into sharing an experience with you. They are putting trust and brand loyalty with YOU! If you have done the work and are vibrating on that higher plane, your charisma will be a magnet to them.

Cracking the Rich Code this way is a very personal journey. You can hire coaches, attend seminars, read more books, and watch videos from thousands of "Been there Done That" experts. Until you do the work uncovering what it means to you, what your obstacles have been until now, and begin to discover YOUR unique gifts, you will not recognize what success feels like! If this chapter has challenged you to dig deeper, I hope you will take the next step and contact me! There's a healthier, wealthier YOU just around the corner!

***

To Contact Beth:

linkedin.com/in/bethrobins4/

Instagram @balancedrobin

facebook
https://www.facebook.com/BALANCEDLIFEPRODUCTIONS/

Beth@balancedlifeproductions.com

Bethrobins.com

Bethinspires.com

Tamara Paul

Tamara Paul is a serial entrepreneur who wears many hats. Author, CEO, Life Coach, Business Coach, Speaker, and more…. Married to former NFL player, Tito Paul Sr., Tamara is a mother of two boys Tito Paul II, and Trey Paul.

Tamara, a graduate of Ohio University, has co-founded multiple companies and is the CEO of Your True Potential. Tamara brings a long track record in successful business management, including financial stability, corporate structure and operational frameworks. An experienced entrepreneur and small business owner, Tamara is the guru of organizational discipline and enablement. In working directly with over 35 companies, launching over 80 new products, as well as having recruited more than 700 superb, self-motivated sales reps, Tamara has made her mark in the business world.

A graduate of one of the most respected life and health coaching programs, Tamara is also a member of the International Coach Federation. She has long recognized her greatest success is in helping others succeed. Her passionate commitment to her work focuses on personal and professional life coaching, health coaching, entrepreneurial/business consulting, work/life balance coaching, and inspirational speaking. Tamara's gift is preparing you for opportunities that are coming your way.

Five "Secret" Strategies for Start-up Business Success

By Tamara Paul

Introduction

In a career well-populated by clients and friends who are start-up entrepreneurs, I have come to understand why some succeed, even dramatically, while more than a few fail. However, success or failure, I've only met a handful who have a clue about even two or three of the five essential start-up business strategies I'm going to discuss. These strategies also apply to launching new products.

In working directly with 37 companies (17 start-up and 30 existing with new products), launching 82 new products, as well as having recruited for my clients more than 700 superb, self-motivated sales reps, I've witnessed companies that struggled out the gate with a business or product launch. I've also witnessed those companies that flawlessly executed their launch—nonetheless, still missed the mark, especially during that all-important initial launch phase of capturing brand recognition and market share.

By carefully analyzing start-ups' varied track records, I have been able to determine the "why" of success or failure, specifically five critical steps every business needs to take in order to succeed. Consider this my "secret sauce"—what I bring to my clients to help ensure success. This is the only path I've found that consistently allows a start-up company, or a company's new product, to "crack the rich code."

These five essential steps include the following:

Harnessing the power of your network

Building a great team at all levels of the organization

Leadership – the driving force behind a great team's success

Selecting the right product or service to bring to market

Marketing through innovative use of social media

Using all five steps is vital, and statistics tell the tale. Thirty percent of small businesses fail within the first year, and 56 percent fail within five years. Clearly, there is room for success, as nearly half of all start-up businesses do succeed . . . but nobody sets out to fail. Following these five code-cracking strategies will help ensure you are among those who succeed long-term.

Stepping away from statistics, I succeeded in my own business by intuitively following these five steps. In teaching these steps to my clients, I have never had a truly successful client who didn't follow, at minimum, four of the five steps. Let's go a bit more in-depth regarding each step.

Harnessing the Power of Your Network

There's a popular saying: "Your network will eventually become your net worth." The key word here is "eventually." Build your network prior to needing it. It took me years to put together a dynamic network of people who were personally committed to my success, I was then able to leverage that network into material success for my own business, as well as for my clients. Without a powerful network, that level of success would not have been possible. When I enlisted my network, they leveraged their own contacts into new prospects for us, often without realizing they were helping us launch our new entrepreneurial venture where everyone wins.

Success in business is impossible without other people. However, "networking" is different than building a network. You almost certainly will use networking tools and skills to build your network while strengthening the commitment of those already in your network, but building a network often involves one-on-one interaction, as well as social media interaction.

A brief, positive phone call or meet-for-coffee get-together can do more to build a network than a thousand email blasts or posts on social media. Get off the internet and actually meet up! Make time for conferences and events in your community. This is where you will find influencers, collaborations, and future team members.

To focus on the difference, creating and nurturing a network is strategic, while networking, especially social networking, is tactical. While one-on-one contact helps define us as humans, some entrepreneurs are afraid to network, and for a couple of reasons:

Competitive product and strategic plan security is hard to balance with keeping a network informed, engaged, and motivated.

From the outside, building a network seems to require a great deal of effort for no immediate or guaranteed outcome.

The best example of this is the discomfort I would feel when I'd meet in a wood-paneled boardroom with a client's C-level team—the CEO, CFO, COO, CIO—the men and women who were making the client "happen." I couldn't help wondering how these people were perceiving me, or worse, judging me. I compensated by over-preparing my work product and my confidence—I never wanted them to see me sweat.

However, experience in more than 100 such C-level client meetings has taught me that they hired me to do what they couldn't do for themselves. That gives me automatic credibility.

When you create your own network, you will be seen as the expert, and your network will not be judging you. Instead, they'll be trying to measure up. That is exactly what those intimidating C-level executives did. They knew I offered something they needed but couldn't create on their own. Rather than judging me, they were striving to make sure I didn't judge them.

Successful entrepreneurs are not afraid of building a solid network. Their skillfully leveraged network is essential to their start-up success.

Building a Great Team at All Levels of Your Organization

When it comes to building a network, try borrowing a classic technique from professional journalists. Every professional news story answers six questions: Who, What, When, Where, Why and How. Your network building must address each of these as well.

Who: Who do you want in your network? Sometimes a single network member can make a huge difference. One client launched a non-profit health education foundation tied to a county hospital; the foundation recruited the chairman of the state's dominant public utility to serve on the board. He made five calls to five of his peers with this simple message: "I am donating $30,000 to this new foundation, paid out over five years, and I would like you, as a favor to me, to match my donation." Each of those C-level executives at major public companies agreed— $5,000 per year wasn't even a rounding error on their balance sheets—and overnight, the foundation was funded for five years, allowing it to focus on creating and delivering health education programs, rather than scrambling for funds.

For start-up businesses, pulling those key leaders together may require the creation of an advisory board of high-end people who give real advice while scouring their own networks for key people who can help.

What: Build a network of people committed to the "cause" behind the start-up, which is why a strongly-worded "mission statement," one without jargon and one with powerful, achievable goals, is essential.

When: Now, of course. No business succeeds by indefinitely putting off their launch, and no business grows in today's marketplace by putting off the creation of their network.

Where: The answer to "where" depends on the start-up. If it is a city-centered business, that's the answer. If the business lives or dies on the Internet, that's the answer. "Where" requires flexibility. McDonalds began as a single fast-food "shack" in California, but it is now the most powerful international fast-food delivery system on earth.

Why? As an entrepreneur, if you have to ask yourself that question, you may not have the passion to make a new company succeed. You need passion and a story behind it. Building a network means attracting others with a shared passion, then enlisting them on your crusade to bring your passion to life. This should involve collaboration rather than competition. Find ways of working together for common-cause goals, tapping into the unique skill-sets of those who come at your shared passion from a different perspective.

Beyond that, as your start-up grows, your network is the obvious place to go looking for the key staff who will make things happen. They already have the passion. They know you, your company, and your product. They care. They want to be part of the process.

How: That will vary based on the company—yours—as well as your product line and your corporate vision. "How" is unique for every company, and is spelled out in every successful start-up's effective, professional, strategic business-and-marketing plan.

Leadership – the Driving Force Behind a Great Team's Success

I have never seen a successful start-up that didn't have an extraordinary leader. Some of these exceptional individuals have unique skill-sets, others know how to pick the right team members, and then stand out of the way. However, these leaders are all visionaries. They can see the future, and are working now to create it.

The success question is "who will lead the company?" One hugely successful web-based business, in operation for 25 years, succeeded because the money-man behind the business got out of the way and let the web designers and product developers do their job. This included the information expert who he handed the company over to once it was launched.

In defining leadership, include:

A clear vision of where the company is going within a competitive marketplace

Decisive decision-making

Integrity and humility; gifts that encourage others to participate in leadership decisions

Positive energy

A consistent pro-active attitude; don't wait for the competition to figure it out, show them what they overlooked

The ability to delegate with grace and confidence

Approachable open-door attitude that makes every team member feel included

With these attributes, a gifted leader can bring along the team, the network, and the marketplace.

Selecting the Right Product or Service to Bring to Market

Some companies are created to bring a specific new product or service to market. However, most successful start-ups set out to create a company able to bring a new mix of existing products to market. Their style and stamina, as well as their integrity and innovation make even an established product seem new and exciting. Their marketing plans are tailored to specific end-users, highlighting what makes the product seem new and exciting, while building on an industry track-record to provide credibility to even the rawest of new products.

Product selection blends the entrepreneur's passion with an exhaustive due diligence. Undertake the three steps below before investing significant time and resources in a vision that seems superficially attractive, but won't succeed in the marketplace.

Use mind mapping . . . brain-dump all possible ideas.

Organize those ideas by category, bringing the mind-map into sharper focus, allowing you to view them all at a glance.

For the two or three "finalist" products you really like, create a Strength-Weakness-Opportunity-Threat analysis. Known in the trade as a SWOT Analysis, this tool creates a four-box matrix, where you list the company's strengths and weaknesses—all of them—as well as the marketplace opportunity when balanced against potential marketplace threats. This will allow you to see how your idea stacks up in a competitive marketplace.

Having culled a great batch of products to find *the* product, it's time to share your product concept or prototype with members of your network. You especially want to engage with the inner circle, such as your Advisory Board. Consider this process an in-house beta test, and one of the most effective ways of getting honest feedback from people you trust. When they offer their opinions, listen to them. This step won't work if you tune out comments that don't agree with your own beliefs.

If your first "beta test" is with actual customers instead of your network, you're begging for negative reviews about relatively minor glitches in your product, and that kind of feedback is hard to overcome. But when the feedback is "in-house," you'll get the benefit of people who are likely to see the big picture, and to give you strategic input without going on the attack to bring you down because they don't like the color of your packaging. When the product goes to market, you'll eventually get that feedback, but don't go seeking it up-front.

If your network has depth, representing a variety of groups who may find your product compelling, you'll discover that your widget did not appeal to a 72-year-old grandmother, but the 41-year-old mother of two was ecstatic about the life changes your product will bring to her and to women like her.

The network beta testers, once they've been heard, can work with you to refine the product. Then, because of their stature in the marketplace, they can also write "launch" reviews, including reviews in the kind of trade journals that count.

The beta testing described here is not a pre-launch effort, it's a PRE-pre-launch effort. It remains within your real or virtual four walls until the bugs are worked out and you're ready for your pre-launch effort, which will include those reviews your network product testers will write for you.

This pre-pre-launch beta testing within your hand-picked network will also help you craft the story behind your product; the kind of story that helps companies win. A classic was, "I liked the razor so much, I bought the company." There are others that have also hit the market like a dynamo, helping to trigger sales growth for new products. While stories can be short, as was that razor example, longer stories also work. These are generally built around aspirational goals for the company and for the product. Make your customers believe that you—and your product—are going to make a difference through the work you do and the people you serve.

Non-profits are masters of this in attracting legions to their causes, because they have legitimate passion behind them. In crafting your aspirational story, you have to duplicate the passion of the most successful non-profits. This may sound daunting, but it's not difficult, as long as your aspirations are real and not just "branding."

Marketing Through Innovative Use of Social Media

There is a world of difference between creating a core network of people who, once committed, will work with you as beta testers, reviewers, advocates at conferences, and who will take other steps to help you succeed. A network of 100 to 250 high-level individuals would be huge, and hugely beneficial. And a network of 25 is not too low to create a powerful impact. However, there is a very different kind of network, which is a "social" network. You won't meet these people. You may never even talk with them. Yet, by connecting with them using Facebook and LinkedIn groups, or via Twitter or Instagram—or even YouTube—you can marshal tens of thousands—or maybe many more—socially-networked individuals who see you as part of their network, and therefore someone they should support, using their own network. You will, of course, be expected to appropriately use your own social network to advance their interests as well.

Every market niche has its own social network. All you have to do is find those networks and capitalize on them. Once you have their attention, it's time to create the buzz.

Search out big companies that you can partner with. Even if you're only a one-person shop, some big companies are looking for partnerships that can enhance their own market position by enhancing yours. Use the social media outlets such as Twitter, Facebook, LinkedIn, and Instagram to find them. Contribute content where it will be noticed, and add more content by partnering with bloggers and influencers who will allow you to engage with their users.

Building your network—and your market—through social media networking is an essential part of even local businesses' marketing strategy. Start by making a list of the movers and shakers in your industry. Who do you want to socially network with? Connect with these people first, and be active on their pages. In other words, "Be Social."

LinkedIn or Facebook can be your social networking starting place. Make a goal to socially connect with 10 people daily. As you grow your social network, be a valuable resource for people. This is not a place to be selling them on your company or product, at least not until you are very well-known. Your social networking goal is to foster a community of like-minded individuals who see you as a thought leader. Some engaging content includes contests, industry insights, eBooks, and how-to videos.

The best piece of advice I can give you is to avoid the hard sell on social media platforms. A pushy sales approach is almost always a turn off.

Every successful social network requires the use of sophisticated and ever-changing social networking tools. Making those tools work requires people with skills and interests different than those of entrepreneurs like you (and always keep that in mind). You're there to serve them, and in doing so, win them over as committed fans. If you try to leverage them to serve you, you're inviting problems.

Conclusion

These five steps are often overlooked or, in the case of "network" and "social network," confused. Sort them out and make them work for you. Do so, and you'll have cracked the "rich code" and—in a marketplace cluttered with visionary failures—you'll be on your fast track to entrepreneurial success.

Next Steps

If you found this helpful, we have more information available, including insider tips on three additional top-secret success strategies: Branding 101, The Sales Funnel Magic and How to Build an email list from Scratch. These are explained in a free course called "Secret" Strategies for Start-up Business Success Part II we offer exclusively for you here: https://my.yourtruepotentialcoach.com/cracking-the-rich-code-main-page/

These resources will help you blast open the door to success! With our help, you can decipher the strategic code that those who succeed—again and again— follow . . . even if they don't always realize it. When you do understand these five steps, you'll find yourself out-performing those who've been doing this right for years. You can do this!

Become a free member to gain access to our business course resource vault: https://my.yourtruepotentialcoach.com/cracking-the-rich-code-main-page/

***

To Contact Tamara:

Website: www.yourtruepotentialcoach.com

Facebook:

https://www.facebook.com/Your-True-Potential-707976349547064/?view_public_for=707976349547064

Twitter: www.twitter.com/YTPotential_

LinkedIn: https://www.linkedin.com/in/tamara-paul-51510457/

Instagram: www.instagram.com/tamarapaul1

Merrilee Sweeney

She's an imagineer, talk show host, author, intuitive relationship expert, counselor, listener, dreamer, solutions expert, and Ambassador of love. Merrilee is a force of nature, in tune, and on a mission to demonstrate and inspire the Power of Love. Her life education is what you always needed but never knew existed. Blessed with an unparalleled understanding of the complexity of life, she is lovingly referred to as the Queen of Hearts. Merrilee is the author, creator and master of "The Game," a manual for personal empowerment and character development, providing an education in love. Her principles apply to every area of life from business to romance, casual to acquaintance. No matter the question, concern, or dilemma, love is always the answer as she describes the rules, the plays, the players and the pieces. Those fortunate enough to learn how to play are destined to experience a life of magic, wonder, and favor. The Queen of Hearts is a living example that love is always the answer.

Merrilee is available for consultation, speaking engagements, interview, and workshops.

The Esoteric Entrepreneur

By Merrilee Sweeney

What does it take to be a successful entrepreneur? Well, that depends on your intention. If you intend to make a lot of money, then education, experience, long hours of commitment, time management, personal sacrifice, a willingness to fail and start over, with a serious investment of time and money are the typical requirements. The acquisition of wealth will also involve a willingness to sacrifice family, health, and self. This is the probable path until you reach the level of income you're striving for, which is more than likely never enough. Unfortunately, many never reach this level of success even after sacrificing so much. However, some do but often they find themselves at the end of their life looking back and asking what was the purpose of all the effort. What does it mean to have the degrees, position, power, accolades, and all the things money could buy if at the end of your life you don't find true happiness?

Please don't fret about being an aspiring entrepreneur or your pursuit of happiness. At some point, we all ponder life and its meaning. But why would someone ponder the meaning of life after they have accomplished the task of getting rich? Maybe because riches and success are not the same thing? Rich is often thought of as financial wealth. Most are looking for the secret key to unlock their financial freedom without considering the cost. They are willing to sacrifice or delay the idea of love to secure their financial footing. Success is much different. Success involves having the ability to honor and maintain loving relationships daily while building a dream. The former is a never-ending pursuit of trial and error, while the latter is a beautiful journey through time, where patience is a virtue, and gratitude brings immense abundance. For me, I have found myself in a place of gratitude every day knowing that I hold the key to my kingdom as I have made the Most High my dwelling.

The entrepreneur...

> "a person who organizes and operates a
>
> business or businesses, taking on greater than
>
> normal financial risks in order to do so."

The entrepreneur defined above is assumed to own a corporate structure or entity of some faction, accepting financial responsibility, money management, employees, and risk management, which is greater than an employee with a paycheck, who is only responsible for his cost of living.

The esoteric entrepreneur takes a different path as this individual's focus is not on corporate structure, money management, or systems. The focus of the esoteric entrepreneur is a vision. He or she is a creator. The desire is not riches, but immeasurable wealth returned in response to value. His or her personal, intrinsic, irreplaceable value must come first.

This comparison may be confusing as both the *traditional* and *esoteric* entrepreneur appear to be the same, but they are very different. The former offers value from a product or service; the latter produces a product or service from the value of the individual. The former experiences competition where the latter has none.

No competition? How can we live in a world with no competition? The answer is simple. The traditional entrepreneur aims to please the population while the esoteric entrepreneur aims to please God. Pleasing the population is a daunting task as new ideas, concepts, desires, and people are constantly changing. Gadgets, styles, and trends are expanding and improving quicker than its production, competition affects pricing, and the fight for market share gets tougher as the population becomes aware of the same wheel being reinvented, but now offered with a shiny new bow. This creative grind is what makes the life of a traditional entrepreneur so daunting.

The constant competition and the personal sacrifices necessary to stay ahead of the game often lead to discouragement, disillusionment, and failure. Why would anyone devote their entire time to a business that could potentially take away their joy, happiness, family life, health, and personal assets for a pipe dream of financial security and free time? I refer to it as a pipe dream because in "man's" world there is no guarantee of financial security. Year after year many people attempt to gain their financial independence, starting and stopping many business endeavors to realize little or no success. The lack of success gets very tiresome and weighs heavily on their spirits. This discouragement makes starting over very exhausting especially with all the time and money lost.

The truth is, our most valuable asset, time, is never returned, or multiplied after it's invested. Time is a one-way investment that one should consider carefully before investing it with anyone or anything. The whole idea of getting rich in the world is a crap shoot, a gamble as years go by whether financial freedom is reached or not. If financial freedom is attained the question becomes, were you able to maintain your loving relationships in the process? If not, the journey wasn't worth the trade. Without loving relationships, money alone will not lead you to your happiness. The esoteric entrepreneur understands that relationships come first. Honorable, loving relationships will lead you to financial freedom while enjoying the journey. Every moment brings an immediate return on your investment. The gift of life is a byproduct of loving relationships. Loving relationships product gratitude for the gifts they bring every day.

As an esoteric entrepreneur, you will discover that *you create joy from creating value within yourself,* then you are a gift to others, instead of being pushed to improve a product or service that can be improved and duplicated by some other. You are the only you. You can produce and sell anything you like, it's not about your product, but rather it's about the value and energy of the individual who offers it. Happiness is your delight when you witness your finances increasing while you effortlessly deliver *your* highest self to others. This is how I have created my world where life has become a dream.

The following personal distinctions are my humble suggestions. Should you be mindful of my direction, it is my conviction that your pursuit of health, wealth, and everlasting happiness will absolutely be yours.

A positive attitude. Whether facing demons, personal challenges, unfortunate circumstances, setbacks, or slim odds, one must always accept that it is only a test. Sustain a positive outlook knowing that your solution is on the way. There is no adversity without an advantage. In other words, you must have faith. *Faith* allows you to smile at the moment, follow your bliss, stay in the present moment and enjoy what is; rather than fear what may come.

Conversely, a negative attitude blinds you from opportunity. Negativity assumes a problem before seeing a blessing. It's the inability to appreciate the good in the present moment of opportunity, which are what dreams are made of, and unfortunately bring negative results in the following moments to come. Displeasure in the present moment is a self-fulfilling prophecy that creates more displeasure. Negativity toward people around us produces anxiety, depression, complacency, lack of fulfillment, frustration, emotional outbreaks, and physical illness. These emotions result in failed relationships and missed opportunities for both love and money. To experience favorable outcomes, one must *let go of all negativity.* Regardless of circumstances, there is always something worthy of a positive attitude.

Vision. For some, the idea of vision may be confusing. The word vision should not be confused with having a plan. To plan is to incorporate time as a marker for goals met. A plan assumes one has control over people, money, and circumstance.

"The best-laid plans often go awry of mice and men."

Robert Burns.

For this reason, many suffer from outbursts of anger, frustration, and contempt as their inability to control their surroundings appear to postpone their success. Relationships are difficult to maintain, and may even be destroyed when plans are thwarted, as frustrations arise when something or someone other than yourself is responsible.

A plan is to *see* the steps necessary to reach a goal. A vision is not a plan because you have no idea how to plan for the accomplishment of your vision. A vision should not be confused with a goal; a goal met is the accomplishment of a step from your plan.

So what exactly is vision? To have a vision is to have a dream so big there is no way you could ever know the plan. A vision is the ability to see in your mind's eye the exact life you intend to live regardless of your current circumstance, lack of knowledge, or lack of money. You don't know how you're going to accomplish it. If your vision is to live in a castle, but your current situation is a small apartment, every day you would walk through your apartment envisioning yourself walking through each room of your castle just as you believe it to be. You would never complain about the apparent reality, for you exist in your castle. Same is true for the esoteric entrepreneur. This individual does not dread the grind of the pursuit, but will instead move through the day as if the vision has already been achieved.

Belief. Belief is often not a consideration as life becomes congested with a never-ending to-do list. Your autopilot is set as each day represents a mixed cocktail of work, chores, errands, kids, friends, activities and if you're lucky, a bit of self-care. We often forget to believe in miracles, answers, solutions, and favor. Instead, many hours are consumed with worry when we rely solely on our own resources. The mind tells us, "If I'm not personally taking care of my needs, schedule, money, business, and challenges, my life will fall apart, and I'll never see success." God's word says, "the key to success is to maintain your relationships above all else." When love is the priority, you'll know that you are not alone in your endeavors. You will work with assurance knowing you know your answer, opportunity, or favor will come through by one of the many relationships you've maintained. After all, we only have each other. How is God to provide an answer if not through one of us, including you? Believe the universe is working in your favor as you work on being your best self to give favor to the world.

Likable. Being likable is no easy task. There are many factors to this virtue. Likability is easily lost as it diminishes each time we are observed negatively managing our challenges. No matter what the situation or circumstance, we always have the choice to remain likable, even when going through extreme situations. If we allow ourselves to be disrespectful, dishonest, outrageous, retaliate, betray, take credit or place blame, we lose trust from those around us. Instead of building a relationship, we have chosen to destroy it. Nobody willfully chooses to befriend or do business with the unlikeable. To be likable, you must be a character of integrity to secure the relationship.

Agreeable. Everybody appreciates approval, even when approval is not being sought. An agreeable nature is much more pleasant and attractive than a disagreeable nature one must endure. When you practice being agreeable before presenting an alternate view, you'll find your audience to be much more accepting of your perspective. An agreeable person is adored and welcomed into many environments, groups, and populations which proves to be of great benefit because the more people you have in your corner, the easier life will be.

Humble. One of the most detrimental faux pas for the entrepreneur is to boast about *being more* or *knowing* more than one does. Even the least experienced person will detect the tone and body language of conceit. Although some may be influenced by this false sense of authority, the truth of their insecurity, masked by arrogance will become transparent, and will ultimately result in a lack of respect from those around him. True and confident authority should never be used as a sword to demean the self-esteem or intelligence of others. To be humble is to exercise modesty of your importance and intelligence with diplomacy. Humility invites trust, making others feel comfortable and encouraged to speak their mind without ridicule. Humility gains love and respect.

Willingness. Everybody loves a team player. The esoteric entrepreneur must be that of a willing heart to do what it takes to fulfill a vision. Look for opportunities to say yes before saying no. Rejection without first acknowledging and accepting what has been offered causes unnecessary discomfort for the opposing party. Rejecting ideas, opportunities, and perspectives from those around you will cause you to be perceived as disagreeable, unpleasant, and in some cases offensive which will have people avoiding you. repelling others will make your success unattainable. A willing heart will appreciate the opportunity to help out, be of service, solve problems, take action, be a leader and persevere where others quit. People love individuals who are willing to help, take initiative, take the lead, try something new, and have an open mind. Try, just try to be easy to get along with first before being disagreeable. There's enough negativity in the world. Be someone who people appreciate having around, one who is willing to enjoy life, get moving, just relax, enjoy good food, have a reason to celebrate, and be merry. Be willing, and you'll be welcome.

Charitable. The law of reciprocity is a natural law, God's law and will not deliver riches to anyone attempting to conduct business with a closed hand. In business, romance, friendship, associates and acquaintances, expect to give in the way of time, effort, money and favor long before you expect to make a profit. Charity may appear to be unnecessary or even contrary to the business-minded, but I suggest you not focus on taking before you learn how to give. The law of reciprocity will make getting rich more difficult and will prolong the end goal if one is unable to discern between a sale and a gift. The esoteric entrepreneur knows this is God's world. To be successful and live in abundance, one needs to prove he's not a victim of the scarcity mentality by giving even when he has little to give. When you give with an open hand without expectation, your charity will be like seeds planted in the field of possibility, coming to harvest when you need it. Your harvest is often multiplied. Be willing to share your gift of service and you will grow in your success. God gives us the gift of favor even when we don't deserve it; we too need to have the same charitable heart. If you want to live in blessing, be a blessing to others.

Honor and **Integrity**. The moment you stop trusting someone, your relationship, business or pleasure is over. These two virtues are the most overlooked personal values plaguing our society today. Because of this, we lack trust and accountability within ourselves. When we don't trust someone's word or deed, we typically make allowances for our own. What is more common is our own bad behavior then blame it on others. This behavior afflicted by many, but there is a silver lining. It's easy to be different, and you can be the difference. With a effort and attention, you can stop blaming others for your shortcomings, and start taking responsibility in keeping your word and deed. This alone will set you apart from the majority and will place you first with opportunities of your desire.

Enthusiasm. Nothing is as infectious as enthusiasm. Everyone wants to know and be around someone who has something to be excited about. Life itself is the essence of positive love energy. When we are full of life and wonder like a child, people are inspired to share and contribute. The esoteric entrepreneur knows that everyone has something to share, but not everyone is willing. Enthusiasm is the key to unlock the treasure of information held within the hands and mind of those within reach. Why? Because enthusiasm is a reflection of love. Love is always a motivator. People love to give and receive love, and enthusiasm invokes the exchange of love.

I, myself have committed to the virtues above. In so doing, I've created a world of favor, guided by divine serendipity. I have never had a plan, only a vision. I've never worried about making money, instead, I focused on planting seeds. I never judged my circumstance, instead, I focused on maintaining my relationships. I've kept myself accountable to God by loving my neighbor regardless of word and deed, money lost, promises broken, and injustices served. I refuse to live by man's truth but instead, by God's promise. I have seen the beauty of the Garden, felt the presence of angels, and experienced the favor only God can provide. Success is to exit a troubled world where the unknown is feared, and instead enter the Garden where the unknown is a welcome mystery that I know for certain is always working in my favor. I never dread the hustle of another day. Instead, I appreciate another opportunity to love and be loved with each rise of the sun. I sleep without worry, and when in need, I ask and it is given at the time *it is needed.*

The answers to my questions, concerns, and dilemmas are always provided. You may find it hard to believe, but this simple recipe has cracked the code to the grandest mystery. "No eye has seen, no ear has heard, no mind can conceive what God has prepared for those who love him," 1 Corinthians 2:9. Him who? Him YOU. Be persistent in your commitment. Be accountable to your word and deed. Enjoy your life and follow your bliss. To love thyself is to crack the rich code.

***

To contact Merrilee:

merrilee@themerrileeshow.com

missmerrilee.com

themerrileeshow.com

www.facebook.com/merrileekleinsweeney

Jason Volpe

Jason has spent the last 25 years helping hundreds of companies transform their business by delivering enterprise class solutions at scale across dozens of industries. Throughout that timeframe, Jason has specialized in all things data, such as *Data Warehousing*, *Business Intelligence*, *Big Data*, *Artificial Intelligence and Machine Learning*. More specifically, he is an expert in business process transformation by infusing data and automation into new and existing processes, making them data-driven.

Today, Jason is a certified *Senior Solutions Architect* at *Amazon Web Services (AWS)* helping customers of all sizes accelerate their business transformation as they progress through their journey of consuming cloud services. Prior to joining *Amazon Web Services*, Jason spent the remainder of his career at *Microsoft*, *Fujitsu Consulting*, *EMC Consulting*, *Nelnet Student Lending*, and *MCI Communications*.

Data Is the New Oil

By Jason Volpe

Ready or not, the democratization of data is here, and it's transforming nearly every aspect of our lives. Data is literally everywhere, and it's fueling a new economy where the currency is the data itself. The birth of the public internet occurred in 1990, and the world has been piling up data ever since. Next year will mark the 30-year anniversary of the internet, yet the last two years show an astonishing trend: **Ninety percent of the world's data was generated within the last 24 months**. It's estimated that 2,500,000,000 gigabytes (GB) of new data is created every single day. The main contributors to this explosive data growth are social media, new devices, the Internet of Things (IoT), and rapid advances in Artificial Intelligence and Big Data.

For marketers, this sea of data is a treasure-trove. For context, let's look at a single tweet's business value to a marketer. Within the metadata of a tweet is the person who posted it, keywords, hashtags, followers, date/time, location, and interests, just to name a few. With this data, I'll create a behavioral personality campaign that groups tweets into two buckets: **1) Psychology** – looks for messaging related to openness, conscientiousness, extraversion, agreeableness, and neuroticism **2) Persuasion** – looks for messaging related to reciprocity, scarcity, authority, fear, and social proof. The reason for separate buckets is both groups are motivated by completely different things. You can use this data to compliment your other campaigns as well. Understanding the behavioral aspect of a tweet can give you tremendous insight into what initiates action by one person vs the other. Circling back to our single tweet example, hopefully, you can see just how powerful this metadata is and what you can do with it.

When you factor in the amount of new data being created, it's hard not to get excited about it all and the various ways it can bring value to prospects and current customers. While 2.5B GBs of new data gets created every day, it's hard to rationalize a number that large.

Let's break that down into areas most people can relate to and see how much new content is being created every sixty seconds[6]. The number of tweets is astronomical. *Over 473,000 every minute. Instagram users post over 49,000 photos/videos every minute. Google conducts over 3.8M searches every minute. YouTube users watch over 4.3M videos every minute, generating massive amounts of new metadata. Netflix steams over 97,000 hours of content every minute. Snapchat has over 2M snaps sent every minute. Facebook Messenger has over 24,000 GIFs sent every minute. Facebook has 510,000 new comments, 293,000 statuses updated, and 136,000 photos uploaded every minute.* Each of these data elements have tremendous value, but when correlated together, marketers can use it to become more data-driven with campaigns that deliver more personalized experiences to customers.

I believe the *impact* of these technological innovations is unlike anything we've seen before. I've spent my entire career focusing on data science and analytics dating back to the early 90s, so you could say that *I dig data*. I've helped hundreds of companies in designing and building large scale data warehouses and artificial intelligence solutions that enable "*informed decision-making*" through reporting and predictive analytics. A data warehouse is analogous to your using financial software to connect to all your financial accounts and then assigning spend categories as new transactions come in each day. Once you have that set up, you can easily see how much you're spending on eating out, monthly bills, or even your daily coffee runs to Starbucks. You could think of this as your own personal data warehouse. It's great at hindsight and demonstrating what's *already* happened. This is really the first step of using data to run your (day to day) business, to know what products are hot, to know which sellers are killing it, or even to know how well you're executing against a strategy or plan. Data warehousing has been the corporate standard for turning *data* into *information* and *information* into *insights* since the 1970s.

Although data warehousing has helped countless companies achieve success they likely wouldn't have achieved otherwise, customers are expecting smarter interactions with the companies with which they do business. If customers perceive your business as "hard to do business with," they'll, more than likely, give their money to your competitor. What do I mean by that? Today's connected customer expects personalized offers and discounts, personalized in-store and online shopping experiences, carefully selected product recommendations, and streamlined communication. Meeting these expectations isn't easy, especially if you're already an established company with business processes that lack integration. Have you ever called customer service for something, spent thirty minutes explaining your situation, only to be transferred to someone else, yet none of the conversation notes were transferred to the new agent? Have you ever casually surfed the web for something you eventually purchased, only to find that same product's ads tracking you on different websites? Most of the time you have no idea who is generating the ads, why they're doing it, or how to get them to stop.

This is referred to as "remarketing," and it's not a mistake. Some remarketing may be perceived as more intrusive than others. However, the bottom line is that it can tarnish a brand if perceived as blind mass marketing or spam. Customers expect companies to use their personal data to provide a much more personalized shopping experience. It's an unspoken agreement between the consumer and the company. When you receive a marketing email that's completely generic, or, worse, is for a product you'd already purchased from the same company the prior month, it reflects negatively on a brand.

Companies have tried to better understand what their customers and prospects want through market research using data sampling, focus groups and surveys. This practice is still used by many companies today. However, not all data is the same. Most of the *new* data being generated is categorized as *"unstructured,"* which is much more difficult to work with. Think of unstructured data as PDFs, emails, videos, web pages, or social media messages. How would you glean any insight from 5,000 videos without actually watching each and every video? How would you identify customer sentiment from 20,000 customer emails? The reality is, you can't. Nor could you hire enough people to sift through that data even if you wanted to. This is where Artificial Intelligence comes in.

Digital Transformation is something you will find on any Chief Marketing Officer's (CMO) top priorities and has been for a few years now. At its core, Digital Transformation is the integration of digital technology (artificial intelligence, machine learning, bots, internet of things, and more) into all areas of a business. In almost every case, this integration touches every business process, many of which will require a complete redesign. It could take some companies years to complete a transformation such as this. Some will feel it's too much effort and cost. Others will feel it's unnecessary because they're already meeting business objectives. Before any final decision is made, it's also important to consider the cost of doing nothing, knowing that many of your competitors are moving towards a customer-centric approach. Start-ups have a significant advantage here because they didn't evolve out of an IT or business organization. They came to market with a product or solution that solved a business problem and are not constrained with existing IT system limitations or processes. The agility of a start-up who can respond to rapid market changes should not be underestimated.

What's important for you, the reader, to take from this is that companies are not the ones driving this disruption. It's being driven by the consumer who needs to feel he's MORE than just a customer number in some database. Customer experience is winning over brand loyalty, and we've seen this occurring for a number of years now. But if you can capture that customer's attention with an intuitive user experience that connects the dots across the different omnichannel processes enabling smart customer interactions, you'll have a business model that's truly disruptive and very difficult to compete with. Disruptive? Yes, because today, it's either "be the disruptor" or "be disrupted". This is true if you're just a one-person company or you have 100,000 employees. The playing field is equalized as it relates to using data that provides a personalized customer experience.

What impact is market disruption having on today's economy? It's astonishing. In 1958, corporations were listed on the S&P 500 for an average of 61 years. By 1980, that average fell off a cliff to just 25 years. The average company tenure dropped again in 2011 to just 18 years. Right now, a company is being replaced about *once every two weeks*. Research[1] now estimates that *75% of today's S&P 500 will be replaced in less than 10 years*. Why is there so much movement today vs 30-40 years ago? Market changes that are brought about by innovation require companies to, at least, evaluate the impact to their current business models. Some companies take a gamble that it's just a fad. Some have a fixed mindset and don't feel a sense of urgency to respond at all. When changes are big enough to disrupt an entire industry's fundamental business models, complacency puts companies at risk of losing their market share and, in the end, going bankrupt. Today's disruption impacts every single industry because it's being driven by the consumers, not the companies nor industries themselves. Buyers are demanding convenience, personalization, and value. Below are a few examples[7] where companies were oblivious to the major disruption their industries were undergoing and paid the ultimate price for it.

Blockbuster - *took in nearly $800M in late fees in 2000; rejected $50M acquisition offer by Netflix who has a $156B market cap today.*

Kodak – *already had a digital camera back in the 1970s but didn't want to cut into revenue coming from 35MM film.*

Borders – *as other brick and mortar book stores expanded their online presence, Borders didn't feel the need to act.*

Tower Records – *could not keep up with digital disruption like music piracy, iTunes, and newcomers like Spotify and Pandora.*

Artificial Intelligence, Machine Learning, Deep Learning, IoT and 5G

Now that you have a better understanding of digital transformation, let's get grounded on what Artificial Intelligence, Machine Learning and Deep Learning are.

Artificial Intelligence is an umbrella for the computer science field solving cognitive functions associated with teaching machines how to understand human intelligence, such as perceiving, reasoning, learning, problem solving, and pattern recognition.

Machine Learning is a collection of *task-specific algorithms* (Models) that run against large datasets with the goal of identifying patterns, predicting future outcomes, or providing product recommendations for upsell/cross sell. If you were trying to identify fraudulent reviews posted to your online store, you would use a fraud detection algorithm. As you add more and more data over time, the model becomes more intelligent as it learns from its experiences. You're essentially empowering machines with the ability to learn and incorporate that *new* knowledge the *next* time it does something. Examples of Machine Learning use cases are *fraud detection within a dataset, finding customers who are at high risk of attrition, and personalizing the customer experience using predictive analytics models to recommend items based on prior customer actions.*

Deep Learning is a subset of Machine Learning that aims at mimicking the layers of neurons in the neocortex of the brain. This is sometimes referred to as a "neural network." Deep Learning uses large datasets as training data so that it can eventually be able to identify more relationships than humans could ever code in software, or even relationships that humans may not even be able to perceive. Unlike Machine Learning, Deep Learning doesn't use human coded algorithms. Deep Learning cascades multiple layers of datasets where each successive layer users the output from the previous layer as input. As it moves deeper through the layers, it becomes smarter and more aware than when it ran within the previous layer. Examples of Deep Learning use cases are *self-driving cars that can understand its surroundings, personalized medicine formulated to a person's actual genome, and learning strategy-type games on its own.* In 2017, a machine taught itself how to play chess. After playing against itself over a million times and learning from each mistake, it figured out how to win every time. How long do you think it took to go from knowing nothing about *chess, shogi,* and *go* to being unbeatable by any human or computer in the world? It took only a matter of hours, and when it played the world's best, it beat the world-champion in *each* of those 3 games.

Internet of Things (IoT) refers to billions of physical devices around the world that are now connected to the internet collecting and sharing data. Good examples of this would be any smart device in your home that is wifi powered, or wearable devices like Fitbits or Apple watches. IoT devices don't have to come from large electronics companies. Millions of people around the world are making their own IoT devices, thanks to products like Arduino and Raspberry Pi. IoT plays a huge role in providing the data necessary to incorporate it into business processes. Manufacturing is a great example of how IoT fits into this. Adding sensors to each machine on the manufacturing line allows them to talk to each other and stream real-time data. If I notice that 20% of the products I'm manufacturing have to be recycled or discarded due to defects along the manufacturing line, I need to know that before the product gets to quality control. By having sensors along the line, millions of attributes can be validated as they progress down that line. Artificial Intelligence and Machine Learning help determine what thresholds would trigger an action, and robotics could be placed at those trigger points so they could move the product from the line and placed in a defect area.

5G – The Internet of Everything will change the world in ways you may not realize. 5G is a new public network that delivers internet speeds that are 1,000 times faster than today's 4G mobile networks with 100 times less latency. It's currently being deployed worldwide and is sure to be the buzz of your town when it arrives. What's also likely to buzz from the new 5G capabilities is your mobile device as you go about your day. 5G will transform devices into real-time beacons that constantly broadcast the exact location of the device, even when it's in motion. Ad load times should be instant which will greatly decrease bounce rates. Click through rates and ROI should see a big boost from 5G as well. One of the biggest changes for advertisers is that, unlike 4G today, data processing can be done at the device instead of remote servers. 4K and 8K video streaming will become the norm, and that opens up a plethora of new advertising scenarios you could not support today. It will be interesting to see how Google addresses its algorithm for page ranking metrics when near-zero latency is introduced with 5G. AI being infused with 5G is really an amazing combination.

My car will soon receive alerts from my refrigerator letting me know I'm out of milk and should hit the store on my way home. As an example, Safeway may decide to send an offer for 40% off organic milk at the location a mile down the road. As I leave Safeway to go home, Exxon may notice that I have an early meeting tomorrow an hour from my house. They know I have enough gas to get to my meeting but not enough to make the round trip without refilling. Sure, they could send me an alert to get gas now, but that's too obvious. No, these guys have data infused into every business process, so you won't get just any offer. They just remodeled the location closest to my office and want to also get me inside the store to see their newest healthy food selection. In addition to a discount on fuel, they also offer me a free rotisserie chicken at that location, which is good through tomorrow evening. The combinations for advertisers are limitless, and it looks to be an exciting world that's right around the corner, from Wendy's and they want to offer me a free Frosty with the purchase of....... See what I mean....!!

Are You Data-Driven

No matter how big or small your company is, staying connected with Industry Trends, Business Journals, Technology Innovation, and understanding how to foster a data-driven culture no longer falls in the "nice-to-have" category. See for yourself. Type "competing on analytics" into a search engine, and you'll see over 41 million results. Companies are using data to differentiate from one another by revolutionizing the way they interact with their customers. Customer offers are becoming much more targeted, personalized, and individually relevant, thanks to the massive amounts of data available. What's different about today's data revolution is the amount of data being infused within business operations and processes today, regardless of how big or small the company is. Have you ever noticed that UPS[4] trucks rarely, if ever, make left-hand turns? Left-hand turns are less fuel efficient, take additional time compared to right-hand turns, and are proven to be less safe for drivers and pedestrians. UPS developed their own real-time routing optimization software that performs 30,000 route optimizations per minute so drivers don't have to figure out their route using only right-hand turns. In estimates provided by UPS, this new data-aware system resulted in a reduction of 10 million gallons of fuel annually ($400M/year), shortened each driven route by 6-8 miles, and reduced total route miles by 100+ million miles annually!

What's GDPR and Can I Really Be Fined by the EU??

By now, you've hopefully familiarized yourself with the General Data Protection Regulation (GDPR) that the European Commission passed into law on May 25, 2018 across all EU member-states. If you haven't, you absolutely need to familiarize yourself with the do's and don'ts of GDPR so you aren't hit with a crazy fine for something that used to be ok but is now considered unlawful. Back in 2012, the European Commission saw the wave of digital transformation coming and, to their credit, **_proactively_** created a plan to give EU citizens control over their personal data, thus building a digital future on a foundation of mutual trust between corporations and EU citizens.

I live in the US, so GDPR doesn't apply to me, right?

Au contraire! GDPR applies to anyone in the world that interacts with the personal data of <u>any</u> EU citizen, even when he's not physically in the EU. Let's take a look at just a few of the impacts. GDPR requires everyone and every business to obtain <u>explicit permission</u> from each EU citizen with whom they interact and the (facilitating) communication channels that facilitate that interaction such as email, phone, SMS, etc. Even if you already have done business with a customer prior to May 25, 2018, you still need to re-request his permission to use his personal data in the manner you plan to use it. Another no-no is using someone's contact information off of a business card that he personally gave you. GDPR does not recognize the exchange of business cards as explicit permission for you to add his contact information to any list or database unless given documented proof of his consent. Indirect op-in methods like using attendee data from a webinar you hosted is no longer allowed either.

For marketers, this has <u>huge</u> impacts. Opt-in forms you use to collect personal data need to explicitly and clearly explain what data is being collected, and how it will be specifically used. If someone registers for one of your upcoming webinars using your opt-in form, he's giving you permission to communicate with him about that particular webinar. If you wanted to use his information for something unrelated to that webinar, you're required to obtain explicit permission to do so. This only scratches the surface of the impacts of GDPR. Google was recently fined in January 2019 for a GDPR violation amounting to over $56M[5]. I know, I know, yes, they have the money. However, small businesses do not, and a fine like that would bankrupt most of them. I think many small businesses would have a hard time surviving an unbudgeted, unplanned $56,000 violation, let alone $56M. Do yourself a favor and get up to speed on GDPR and adjust your business processes accordingly. It's only a matter of time before the US puts legislation in place similar to what the EU has done.

Official GDPR Link: https://gdpr-info.eu

Want my personal data for your marketing campaigns? Pay me for it!

Consumers are flipping the script on big businesses thanks to a little help from GDPR. Creative start-ups have jumped on this data privacy revolution. Personal data exchanges allow consumers to *opt-in* and be compensated for allowing their personal information to be used by companies. Personal privacy is a hot topic in the news today for good reason. Social Media sites are competing for your undivided attention at all times of the day. It's important to keep in mind that these platforms are being provided to you free of charge. They don't make money by you *using* their platform. However, they DO make money letting advertisers know *how* you're using their platform. The things you do on these platforms helps advertisers provide relevant content that you find valuable. What we're seeing today is a growing movement of the monetization of personal data driven by the consumers of platforms such as social media. As 5G becomes more widely deployed, this will become an area you will definitely want to keep your eyes on. It will not only change the business models of these giant tech companies, it will also shift a reasonable amount of power *from* them and move it *to* their end users. GDPR is really only the start of what is likely to be a worldwide movement of fair and safe use of an individual's right to privacy. The internet has been the wild west for decades but this focus around data privacy is real. How will this impact all of us who use these platforms? That will squarely depend on how these platforms embrace having to potentially pay for something they've never had to pay for but consider their Intellectual Property. Don't anticipate this transition being painless anytime soon.

To contact Jason:

Email *jason@AreYouDataDriven.com*

Website *http://www.AreYouDataDriven.com* if you'd like any additional information.

Endnotes

1   Digital Transformation Is Racing Ahead and No Industry Is Immune [DXC Technologies via Harvard Business Review, 2017]

2 Epic Fail: How Blockbuster Could Have Owned Netflix [Variety, 2013]

3 A/B Testing and Beyond: Improving Netflix Streaming Experience with Experimentation and Data Science [Netflix Tech Blog, 2017]

4 Why UPS trucks (almost) never turn left [CNN, 2017]

5   Google Fined €50 million for GDPR violation in France [The Verge, 2019]

6 Data Never Sleeps 6 [Domo, 2018]

7 Companies That Went Bankrupt From Innovation Lag [Investopedia, 2018]

Knicole Burchett

Born and Raised in the Northwest, Knicole enjoys the simple things in life. Her zest for life is contagious for all those around her as she gives hope and inspiration to so many to achieve their dreams. She is an independent and successful mother of two boys who keep her moving. After graduating from college and entering the corporate working world she quickly learned the value of time freedom and has been on a mission of paving her own path of entrepreneurship. Along that path, she found the industry of network marketing and a breakthrough product that has allowed her to change thousands of lives while living on her own terms. After finding this success, she became determined to lead the way for others to achieve this freedom. It has become her goal, passion, and mission to help as many people as she can along the way. She is known for her personality, genuine love for others, and encouragement she shares every day. Outside of spending time with her family, you can find her jet setting and experiencing the world. We never know where she will be going next.

My Journey to Time and Financial Freedom

By Knicole Burchett

Sitting there in my cubicle, it was the summer of 2013, and I was about 6 months pregnant with my second child. As I looked out the window on that beautiful sunny summer day, I watched my boss leave the office AGAIN for another day of golf. He had no problem coming to the office in his golf attire and letting us all know it was a golf day. I use to day dream what it would be like with that power, to have that kind of freedom of getting paid, soaking up that natural vitamin D and feel the sunbeams against my face. I always wondered what it would be like to "work" from the golf course, the river, or some exotic island. For the past 10 years I had worked for someone else. I was programmed by society that this was the way of life. Don't get me wrong, I had an amazing insurance career, I was successful, winning company awards and trips, but I was trading my time for money. Materially, I had everything. I had a nice house, a nice car, a boat, and I could buy my children anything they desired. But deep inside, I felt empty. I felt there was more to life. What are all of these things if I didn't have time to enjoy them? Why and how do I become the Boss who has this time freedom? These are the thoughts racing through my head as I watched him leave. Something happened inside me on this particular day as I opened up another email denying my request for time off. This was not just any request, my father was flying in for the weekend for the big gender reveal for my second son, Kole. I was all too used to missing things because I had to work. That email denying my time off hit me hard but was exactly what I needed. I had literally had enough!! Tears begin pouring down my face, and it was like the person inside me was breaking free. I always knew there was a better way. Growing up, my mother was always home and dinner was on the table, she did not have the stress of working as the family was able to live on my step father's salary. Being a single mom it is much different, I was the one income. I had been working 40-50 hours a week since college graduation as was drilled into me as the way of life. I could have just been thankful and content I had the "dream job" and could provide for my kids, but all I felt was guilt. Guilt of not being around and guilt of missing so much time with my family.

I was ready to give it all up for my time and freedom, having money was nothing without my time. Reality flashed right before my eyes. I had missed so much of my older son's childhood. Daycare had raised him. My memories of him consisted of rushing him through life. Rushing him to get dressed, to eat breakfast, rushing through traffic to drop him off to daycare then back to pick him up and rushing him to eat dinner and get ready for bed, to only do the same thing the next day. The little free time I had with him, I had to split with his father. His whole childhood felt in a hurry and in that moment of being denied time off, all I thought was "here we go again", I wondered how can I be so blessed with another child if I couldn't give my all?

My older son was struggling in school, he was struggling not having me around and he was struggling socially. I wasn't there for him like a mom should be. I was that mother that was getting calls from the Principals office every other day. My son was always acting out, being defiant, destroying property and school work, starting fights and disrupting other kids, you name it he was doing it. The Doctors labeled him ADHD and put us through the ringer of trying to find a prescription that could "fix" him. I tried anything and everything to help him, from medications, counseling, surgery's, bio feedback, diets and supplements, I was desperate for answers for his special needs and not being able to give more time to him tore me apart. I could not even imagine bringing another child into this chaotic life. I don't know what came over me, but I stood up from that cubicle, started pacing back and forth, then straight over to the manager, I told her I was leaving and not coming back. I wanted to give notice but because of access to proprietary information I had to be walked out on the spot. No time to even change my mind. I stood there hysterically and packed up my desk.

As I walked out of the office and out of my comfort zone, I really didn't know whether to laugh or cry. I didn't know how I was going to make my rent or car payment, but I didn't care. Many emotions were flowing through me but all I could feel was relief. I was not going to let someone else raise my new baby and I was done trading time for money. I had a WHY so big I knew I could conquer the earth to achieve it. My dream was simple. I just wanted to be able to stay home and be around for my boys and I was willing to sacrifice everything to make this happen and I know I would do whatever it took. I share this story because we all hit breaking points. It's what we do in those times to never give up finding a way to make your dream a reality. Society never taught me entrepreneurship or how to own my own business or how to make residual income. I didn't even know the first step to take, but I felt that freedom existed. I felt it existed because I was in sales and sales allowed me more than an hourly wage and set salary. It allowed me to work harder and achieve more. I would have never been content knowing exactly what I would be earning that month. I had to have the option to do better. It was in my blood.

Leaving my career was scary, but I hit the internet to research how to start a business and how to work from home. Through this I found the world of network marketing. I found groups of people who had it figured out, or like me trying to figure it out. I began to join in and copy others, but I was failing. I was doing it all wrong and people were not afraid to let me know. Yes, I was that person that would spam my business on your page or inbox. It was not working and I almost quit so many times. I had zero experience in the network marketing world and it was so confusing for me, but I could see people having success and I was determined to learn. I began to connect with those people. I saw this quote "people follow people they know like and trust." A light bulb went off in my head. It was no different in the online world than it was connecting in person or on a sales call, I knew how to do this. I needed to build relationships, just like I did every day at my job. My entire approach changed. I was no longer posting my websites, sales of my products or spamming inboxes. I began sharing about my life story. Sharing the journey of my new born child, sharing the daily struggles with my ADHD son, and sharing the sacrifices I was making to be able to be home for my boys. I wanted people to get to know me, and I wanted to know them. It's hard to be vulnerable and let people in, but I knew I had to do this to make it in this industry. The more I shared, the more friends I made online, the more people reached out to me, thanked me, followed me, and told me I was inspiring them. It became addicting. From that point on everything changed. I spent the next couple years online just building relationships, connecting with people, caring about who they were and learning their desires. I developed a massive following for the many single moms who dreamed of staying home with their kids and being able to do what I do. That became my drive, my purpose and desire. I wanted to help as many as I could to achieve this. I learned quickly that the more people I helped reach their goals the better we would all be. Your goal might not be to stay home with your kids but we all have some goal. Maybe it's being able to take care of a parent, or travel, or buy a home. Whatever it is, you can create a following of people who will relate to you by sharing your story.

As I head into my 5th year of online marketing people always ask me my secret. My secret of how I have built teams of thousands of people with no marketing experience, my secret to happiness, and my secret to turning things into gold. I am not a great speaker. I do not make perfect videos. I am not good with technology, I do not have a marketing system, and I'm not even close to the marketers who I look up too. I am just me. My success comes from being open and sharing my journey, my desire to help people is also at the top of the list but it also requires the right attitude. Your perspective is everything. You cannot always control the outcome of what happens, but you can control how you look and react to it. I always try to find the good in people and in every situation. I try to keep anything negative out of my surroundings and out of my voice at all times! Another key to my success is setting small reachable goals and always have something to strive for. My first goal was to make enough to be able to afford my basic bills so I could be home with my boys. If I could pay my rent, utilities, and get food on the table, I was good. Once I achieved that milestone, my second goal was that I wanted to become debt free. I started paying off my college loan and credit cards. My third goal was to save enough to buy a stable home for my boys so we did not need to keep moving around as renting was not easy as we always had to uproot and worry what next. By my third year of network marketing I was able to sneak into the six figures and reach this goal. I bought them their first home. I knew if I was consistent that if someone like me could do this, then anyone could. Everyone's journey is different. We have to try not compete and compare ourselves to one another, but rather work on ourselves to be better every day. What took me 3 years to accomplish might take you three months or five years. Just never stop sharing YOU and your story. Let people get to know you so you can build a genuine following. When you have that, you can join and share any company, service or product and have success, because you have developed a trusted network.

As much as I wanted my first networking company to be my only company and legacy, I quickly learned that in this industry, "the only thing that stays the same is everything changes". I learned nothing is guaranteed to be there tomorrow, just as your job in the "real world" is not. It's also not guaranteed that your chosen company will always align with your beliefs and vision, they may change ownership, they may change their products, their pay plan, and even their rules. In my case, my first company in this industry sold out and disappeared, and my second company changed their rules which made it more difficult to earn. I learned very quickly it wasn't a company or a product that would determine my future, it was me. One thing I did have leaving those companies was my relationships with people. Starting over was not hard because of the people around me. They became my friends, and my family. We had similar mindsets and goals, they kept me going when my "real life" friends frowned upon my chosen path. I knew if I always focused on helping people I would always be OKAY! I learned to brand who I was and not just a company or name. I also learned to always support people and not burn bridges. I love seeing people succeed and love cheering them on, even when it's not on my team. I am grateful for all my experiences. For all the people it brought into my life. I learned about what I wanted in a company and what I didn't want. This industry allowed me to try many things. I was on a constant search for a product to help my son's struggles and I went from company to company seeking answers. Then one day, I found the product that completely changed his life. Sadly, it was not a marketing company, I could not join them and share. I would of had to move to California and join their corporate sales team. That did not stop me, this product was so amazing I could not keep quiet. I shouted as loud as I could to all my following what this product had done for me. I contacted the leader of that company and told them, if they were to ever open up a marketing side I wanted to be the first in line. For months I documented my results of this product and told the story of my son and his struggles and breakthrough when nothing else had worked. Then one day I got the call, "Knicole, we are opening up a marketing platform and you are the first to know. I dropped everything else I was doing and since that day have been dedicating the last couple of years educating people and changing lives. It has become my passion. Testimonies of lives changing still hit my inbox daily and it is more meaningful and rewarding than anything I have ever been part of.

My journey has been guided and led me to this exact place in life. I could share every detail, timing, and how one thing lead to another but I will save that for another chapter. The struggles I went through with my son had a bigger purpose. His years and years of counseling, different medications, and struggles no longer exist because of this product. It has become my passion and life's purpose to share, educate and help as many people as I can get their hands on this. Society did not teach us time freedom, and it definitely did not teach us the amazing benefits of this product. Finding this was not by chance, and what a better way to share than through network marketing. Since sharing our story, we have created a movement across the world of helping others. We help them with their health, their time freedom, family freedom, and financial freedom. The industry I have found has unlocked the key to greatness and expected to grow over 200 percent in the next few years. This breakthrough product is not going away, and there are not many chances in a lifetime where you can jump on a trend that is changing the world. I have never been more passionate or more ready to lead this mission. I feel it inside that I was actually put in this world to lead this charge.

Do not ever give up on your dreams, no matter what they are. My dream was simple, to be home for my boys and help my son Jimmy heal. Since walking out of my corporate career that sunny golf day, I have never looked back. I have never had to put my youngest son in daycare and my older son is now thriving because of this online journey. Even though my younger son just turned five and starts school full time this year, I still could not imagine working for anyone else. I have grown to love the laptop lifestyle where I can work from anywhere in the world, connect to anyone in the world and be able to do it on my own schedule and my own terms! I cannot promise roads will not change in my future, but I can promise I will never stop working on myself and growing my brand and sharing what I believe in. Whatever your passion is, keep going. Keep inspiring others with your story and mission. There was nothing super special about me back then, I am just someone who never gave up.

If you find you are at a place in life looking for a change, looking for meaning, for better health, or looking for time freedom, I would love to connect. I have so much more of my story to share. Thank you for giving me that opportunity to continuing doing what I love, which is inspiring others to help achieve their desires.

***

See you at the Top,

Knicole Burchett

To contact Knicole:

knicolejenae@gmail.com

website: knicoleburchett.com

phone 3602811314

Facebook: fb.me/knicolejenaeburchett

Phil Bristol

Phil Bristol, the Founder, President, and CEO of Projectivity Solutions, works with boards of directors, executives, leaders, high-potentials, and teams to increase their effectiveness, influence, and profitability. He helps facilitate personal and organizational change, serves as a sounding board on complex people issues and works with top performers so they advance to the next level of responsibility. Projectivity Solutions, Inc. helps businesses increase growth and profitability while solving the multi-generation challenge of family-owned businesses. Facilitated solutions help owners develop and communicate a customized "Gold Standard" that creates and sustains a culture trust-based high performance. Phil is passionate about helping people and organizations move to new levels on their journey. In doing this, he uses his practical business techniques and tools, expertise in interpersonal skills, communication, critical thinking, business strategy, and execution to produce pragmatic results. His approaches integrate 130 years of research in business, organizational development, and people skills into each engagement. He is an entrepreneur and leader with over 35 years of business experience and has run a successful company for over 25 years. His presentations and workshops are acclaimed by executives worldwide.

Cracking the Growth Code:

The Greatest Economic Engine Faces the Greatest Challenges

By Phil Bristol

There are not enough people running companies today who can lead them to grow.

The number of employee size in American businesses is shrinking and the yearly business mortality rate remains constant. Small businesses in the U.S. account for 99.7% of the economy, 60% of employment and 78% of new jobs. Yet, according to Jim Clifton, chief executive of Gallup, Inc., the U.S. economy has more business deaths per year than business births. Currently, there are six million companies with payroll and employees. Of those six million, about a million are "small businesses" with five to 10 employees. Unfortunately, U.S. Bureau of Labor Statistics shows that about 20 percent of these "small businesses" will fail within their first year. By the end of their fifth year, roughly 50 percent will fail. And after 10 years, the survival rate drops to approximately 35 percent. To avoid business mortality and diminished profitability, a CEO needs to have a realistic business plan and a motivated team. Clearly, cracking the code to survival is even more relevant today if small businesses are going to grow, have success, and longevity.

Measures for Success

A business typically begins because of the founder's passion and entrepreneurial spirit and then grows organically with increased customer demand. In the early years, the leader's vision and expertise is the dominating mindset that drives profit. The ability to set an appropriate pace and communicate direction begins to create a culture of success. Equally important is allocating time to work

ON the business not just IN the business. This is the ability to identify and focus on specific issues that are creating obstacles to growth. Removing these barriers significantly improves a company's performance. What you can name you can measure, and what you can measure you can improve.

Focus on Essentials

The three critical components for sustained success are profit, process, and people. Nothing will disrupt performance, productivity and profitability quicker than poor staff morale. People who are unhappy check out. A recent Gallup poll shows that 71% of employees are actively disengaged and 53% are just plain unhappy! The majority of issues with employee morale and staff voltage are created by inept leaders and managers who are not doing the job they were hired to do. While revenue, cash flow, cost structure, product/service quality, and customer satisfaction are paramount to marketplace viability, the owner mindset is indispensable in order to create a lasting competitive advantage.

Owner Mindset

Owner mindset and staff voltage create the foundation for long-term competitive advantage. This is critical because mindset is grounded in emotional intelligence. In *Primal Leadership* (Daniel Goleman, 2004) Goleman highlights self-awareness as the most important of the four domains of Emotional Intelligence which is commonly referred to as Emotional Quotient (EQ). Goleman goes on to say ".... self-awareness facilitates empathy and self-management and is the foundation for effective relationship management. Leadership, then, builds from a footing of self-awareness." The other three spheres include self-management, social awareness and relationship management. All four of these domains are key in a leader's influence on company culture. Leaders with high EQ are more self and organizationally aware, they mentor the development of others, and foster collaborative team work. An emotionally intelligent leader has the capacity to appropriately influence and motivate others. This is the core to cracking the performance code.

The Six Leadership Styles in a Nutshell

VISIONARY - moves people toward shared dreams when changes require a new vision, or when a clear direction is needed. This style has a strongly positive effect when applied appropriately.

COACHING - connects what a person wants with the organization's goals, and helps people improve performance by building long-term capabilities.

AFFILIATIVE - creates harmony by connecting people to each other, heals rifts in a team, motivates team members during stressful times, and strengthens connections

DEMOCRATIC - values people's input and gets commitment through participation by building buy-in and getting valuable input from employees.

These four styles have a strongly positive cultural impact when applied appropriately.

PACESETTING - leans into challenges and sets goals to get high-quality results from a motivated team. However, the impact on culture can be negative with too much emphasis on speed and conflicting messages.

COMMANDING - soothes fears by giving clear direction in an emergency. This style can be effective in a crisis, to kick-start a turnaround, or help with problem employees. When used too frequently, this style becomes highly negative.

Focus on People

The CEO-Owner mindset establishes the organization culture and how people are treated. The manner in which staff is treated creates staff "voltage" - the energy in the work place that reflects the level of enthusiasm and the intensity of focus as expressed by the people working in that company.

You can feel staff voltage when it's high and sense it when it's low. In your company what does it feel like? Is there a sense of purpose?

Are people interacting? Are they intensely focused? Do you hear laughter? Or do people avoid talking to each other? Are doors closed? Do quiet conversations stop when you walk by?

There are three determinants of Staff Voltage:

1. Leadership – is staff communication good or non-existent?

2. Healthy and consistent inquiry by staff – are questions treated as criticism? Are defenses up making little problems into big issues?

3. Work clarity – do people understand the key results they are accountable for and how they are expected to treat each other?

Don't kid yourself that 'you just need people to do their jobs' and you can run a successful company. You need people engaged and your staff to care.

Voltage is one of the most important predictive performance barometers a company can use in managing the workplace culture. When the staff starts to own the voltage of the company, when they see the impact it has on productivity and customer experience, a subtle shift happens in the organization.

Voltage often starts with staff being given a chance to express their feelings and perceptions about the company in some form of survey or assessment. While getting staff feedback can be uncomfortable for leadership, it's a critical component in creating a culture where employees feel valued, listened to and respected. Staff morale and staff voltage are the responsibility of every manager in an organization and that responsibility starts with the leader.

The reality is that most people spend more time interacting with people in their work environment than they do with their family. That makes the success of a work community a high priority for any business leader. Studies validate that when people feel good about their job, about their manager and about the work itself, they are more productive. More productive employees mean better results - higher margins, better performance and a positive impact on customers. Unhappy or disengaged employees have a negative impact on every aspect of your business. Exceptional employees dislike working with them and also question the reason management keeps these employees on staff. Customers will come into contact with a disengaged employee at some time, and they will remember that encounter longer than they will remember an encounter with an exceptional employee.

By being proactive in creating a culture where employees feel valued, know their ideas count and feel empowered to make decisions that contribute to the well-being of the organization, a business leader is allowing the company the opportunity to not just survive but to thrive.

Focus on Direction and Process

Has the CEO articulated the company vision, obtained buy-in to the organizational mission and created with employees the company's shared core values? When a company is just getting started there is huge energy created by the excitement of starting something new. The people on the team at these early stages of growth were selected based on their belief in the CEO.

They were energized by the CEO's vision of the product or service. Not many processes or procedures were in place. Everyone simply pitched in and did whatever it took to get a product out the door and deliver outstanding customer service. The company in these stages of growth is CEO-centric. It is the business leader's passion, vision and energy that keeps the company on a path for growth.

According to the research conducted by James Fisher (*Navigating the Growth Curve*, 2006), by the time a company has grown to over 20 employees, the dynamics have changed dramatically. The company has to shift to enterprise-centric, allowing processes to take the place of figuring things out as they go. People must have clear roles and responsibilities so they understand their value and how they contribute to success. For a business leader who has been in total control of every decision, who has been the go-to person for almost everything, to suddenly have to start delegating and letting go of some of that control is extremely challenging. The willingness and ability of the CEO to develop key leaders and delegate decision-making is required in order to shift from being CEO-focused to growing as an enterprise.

As a company moves beyond the early stages, communications become increasingly difficult, especially if systems aren't in place that help drive how work gets done. A study by Bain and Company indicated the organizations that have clearly defined vision-mission statement outperform those who do not.

In order to make sure leaders know what systems and procedures are needed, the CEO has to have a plan that outlines how the company is going to grow. This plan should answer questions like:

- Are you planning on expanding into other states or countries?

- How do you deliver your services from multiple locations?

- What skills will you need as you grow?

There's a tendency when there is a tenfold increase in activity levels within a company for leaders to start throwing people at the activity. The irony is that when they do that they actually create a more complex organization that is more difficult to manage because complexity increases for only one reason: the addition of people (Fischer, 2006). As a result of throwing people at the problem, the company ends up in another stage of growth before it is ready. The company struggles even more because the necessary systems to build a suitable infrastructure to handle this new level of complexity has not been created.

It's much easier to decide something is a "people issue" than to determine it's a "process issue". If, for example, clients are complaining that it's taking too long to hear back from the company when they lodge a complaint, leaders may assume that the person in charge of customer service is at fault. Leaders may think they should just hire another customer service person because that won't be as expensive as implementing a CRM system.

As with many other aspects of growing a successful business, the CEO needs a plan. The leader needs to know what systems are important for the company, but the leader won't know that unless he/she has run a similar company or looked for outside expertise or hired experienced managers who have the knowledge to at least understand the problem.

Focus on Profit

The two critical activities a business must focus on in order to create a sustainable business model are increasing profits and decreasing costs.

A business must focus on both gross profits and net profits, and each one requires a consistent and well thought out strategy. Understanding both allows leaders to make better business decisions. But ignoring the basics that drive profits is the primary reason businesses fail.

It is also imperative that organizations are disciplined in their approach to generating profits and that all employees have a basic understanding of how their job, and the work they do every day, helps the company make and keep its financial stability. This means that companies must continually evaluate and understand the metrics behind why they price their product and service as they do. The goal is to continually maximize profit margins.

Leaders must also continue to strategically analyze current, as well as projected, profit rates and compare them with business plans for the next one to three years in order to be prepared for the capital investments needed in the future.

Business leaders that use their balance sheets and income statements to make decisions earn 60% more than their peers, and their businesses are up to 45% larger. Similarly, leaders that track business metrics at least monthly earn 60% more than their peers, and their business is up to 80% larger.

Business plans and budgets must be dynamic to changing business conditions. Simply driving revenue does not guarantee success. Nor is an exclusive focus on top line revenue a plan for growth. Without a solid understanding of how much money it takes to operate, a company will go out of business.

That's why successful companies recognize the importance of creating a profit plan (aka budget) - a 12-month view of the company's core competencies from which they derive revenue, monthly projections of revenues, cost of goods and expenses.

By understanding cost of goods and how much gross profit is made on each product or service, a company can evaluate and make better decisions as to where to allocate its resources. As an inclusive process, having all company employees understand how their jobs impact the company's ability to make money, those employees see the value they bring to the organization. When employees feel valued, they become engaged. Engaged employees boost productivity, performance and profitability. Everyone comes out a winner.

Profit Design

A company's profit design starts with understanding that profitability is a result of the leaders managing and tracking a complex, interdependent set of components that contribute to the company's financial performance. This challenge is all about making sure the company is testing all assumptions on a regular basis and sharing this information within the business.

The way in which information gets distributed throughout the company can either improve profitability or lower profit margins. The easier it is for someone in the organization to get access to the critical information, the easier it is for them to succeed, which will end up making the company more profitable. So to succeed, companies also need an effective knowledge management system

Most CEOs understand the need for a business plan. However, too many are not aware of the fundamental profit design of their business, including the essential rubrics for creating profitability. Before a business plan is developed, CEO's should consider the following twelve factors that impact a company's profit design:

1. **Value Exchange** – The profitable organization and exchange of value for money.

2. **Customer Intelligence** – The informed awareness of who the customers are and what they want.

3. **Scope** – The range of product or service offered.

4. **Business Development** – The fusion of targeting, capturing and caring for the customer.

5. **Strategic Control** – The unique power of your offerings.

6. **Strategic Allies** – The specific external partners engaged to expand sales.

7. **Knowledge Management** – How a company leverages its unique knowledge.

8. **Culture** – The landscape and focus of the human workplace community.

9. **Organizational Structure** – The organizing of people to successfully complete tasks.

10. **Operating Systems** – The support structure for critical enterprise processes.

11. **Research and Development** – The continual discovery of solutions to the customers' needs.

12. **Capital Intensity** – The measurement of required financial resources.

Cash is King

Cash is cash, and revenue is revenue. They are not the same thing. More than one company has closed its doors drowning in revenue, unable to pay its bills. Cash flow is simply understanding how much money a company has every day or every week to pay bills, which is critical in keeping the company afloat.

A company never has too little cash to track. Business leaders who believe they'll start tracking cash when they have some are in denial of the reality of what cash flow management is all about. There is nothing more important than understanding how fast the cash is coming in (or not coming in) and how fast cash is leaving the business. In fact, understanding cash flow can help leaders make better decisions up to six months in advance. By really paying attention to how cash is flowing in and out of the business, the CEO can leverage even a small amount of cash, and sometimes, in the early stages of any business, that's all there is!

Critical questions to ask:

- Does the company have a profit plan?
- Does the company monitor cash flow?
- Does the company have an operational plan?
- Does the company have a marketing plan?
- Does the CEO pay attention to financials?

The real value in managing cash flow is in reality, not in wishing money will come through the door. You may have to push out payables if the receivables are a bit weak for that period of time. But by tracking cash flow weekly or every other week, there will be no surprises. The value of a cash flow projection will also keep the leader focused on the one critical activity he/she has to be focused on – essential financial health.

Following the Money!

Knowing how important cash flow is to a business helps a business leader send a positive and productive message to staff. If employees see the relationship that workflow (i.e. how work gets done in the organization) has on billing, they will better understand the urgency for getting projects or products out the door on schedule.

A project or product that isn't getting shipped on time means the customer isn't going to be paying any time soon. The reality of how one person's job impacts a company's ability to generate cash is powerful. Don't assume employees won't understand that relationship. Teach them how valuable their part is of the process.

Once the business starts to generate a larger amount of income, don't assume all is okay. Cash flow management should always be a part of the leader's job. There may be an accountant or bookkeeper that runs it for the CEO, but he/she should always know how much cash the company has.

In Summary

Ultimately, cracking the code to sustained success is measured by profitability and marketplace viability. But profits alone are not maintainable without productivity, which is not workable without having the right people, in the right position, communicating, and working as a team. So the simple goal of maximizing profits is not the best measure of financial success.

The CEO's mindset shapes the culture for a lasting competitive advantage. How each leader treats their direct reports creates voltage. David Maister's (*Practice What You Preach*, 2001) research has proven there is a causative relationship between staff voltage and a superior customer experience and quality service delivery. Yes, strategic and operational clarity is needed, yet without trust-based relationships any team will have a reduced capacity to resolve disagreements and gain commitment. As organizational complexity increases, CEOs must lead with a situationally appropriate style and knowingly prioritize the focus of the company on profit, people, or process.

LINKEDIN: www.linkedin.com/in/philbristolcmcpmp/

TWITTER: www.linkedin.com/in/philbristolcmcpmp/

WEBSITE: www.projectivity-solutions.com

Missy Grohne

Missy is an adventurer at heart. She loves to explore, to ponder and experience each day to its fullest capacity. Her journeys never cease. She has had the opportunity to travel the world experiencing various lifestyles, foods and challenges. Her spirit goes with the wind allowing her to enjoy jobs from sailboat bum, school teacher, adventure guide, voice over artist, film maker, laser consultant and network marketer extraordinaire.

Missy was born in Illinois and grew up in "The Swamp", as the family referred to the creek in the backyard.

She now lives in New York City with an attack bird and enjoys hiking in the Catskills, Broadway shows, sailing, and finding the out of the way quirky shops hidden in the most fun places in the city.

The Hike, The Adventure

By Missy Grohne

"Two roads diverged in a wood and
I took the one less traveled by,
And that has made all the difference."

Robert Frost

People love telling you what you should want, what you should or should not do and there is no way in thunder you can be a success if you buy into that. People who do not understand what you are doing or have a fear of stepping out of the safe zone of their norm will do their best to let you know you won't succeed. But for every one of them, there are hundreds more who are ready to "take the road less traveled by" and see the difference. I have laid out plans to help guide you around the pitfalls and bogs laid by the naysayers. These are people you can distance yourself from, then you can reach the top of your potential with leaps and bounds and find the financial success you seek.

My parents always laughed when they would remember me as a baby flailing my left arm out and just saying "Noooo" when I did not want to be told what to do or conform to the norm. As I got a wee bit older I used to sometimes feel a need to take a day off from kindergarten (back then the principal was understanding) to go out into the backyard to study ants and spiders and explore the giant world of my backyard. Such treasures there were to be found and the occasional bumps and scrapes were badges of honor. This was something I wanted to do and I was not told I could not do it. Curiosity and a sense of adventure into the unknown was a part of me and I am sure I tried experiments on ants that may be frowned upon today by the Save the Ants foundation.

Aside from skipping a few days of kindergarten to follow a desire, I was also inspired by the movie "The Sound of Music." I believe I saw it 36 times when it came out. I literally had it memorized but two key songs described me well, although I was too young to see it. "How do you solve a problem like Maria" (substitute "Melissa" because I need two syllables) and "Climb Every Mountain." I got chills with those songs then and they still resonate in my ears and heart when I hike in upstate New York. I "I climb every mountain; I ford every stream." I try something new and do it with passion.

Basically, I was and am ME. I love the excitement (key word) that a new challenge brings.

Right out of college I decided that sailing in the Caribbean would be more fun than getting a traditional job. Eight of us went. Seven knew nothing about navigation. I was the only one who was an expert sailor.

We all took a course in ocean navigation, got certified and rented a 36' Carib sailing boat. We were carefree and the time there was loaded with adventure and passion (key word) for what we were doing and we loved our "job". We became entrepreneurs. We found ways to make extra money to buy the staples we needed on the boat.

I did come home to a stable job. It had benefits, four walls, long hours and a steady paycheck. But my sense of adventure lurked in the background.

I became a tour director and traveled all over the United States and Canada. It would have been easy to stay the course and keep my job with all sorts of security attached but could I dare to take the chance and do what my instinct and passion told me I would be happier doing?

A few years in the travel business I was offered a coveted position to become a helicopter hiking guide in the Canadian Rockies. I did not know anything about how to do this but I never took a look back. If you do need to look back, make it brief and use it as a stepping stone towards progress.

I could literally climb every mountain and ford every stream so I jumped right in. It would have been easy to find an excuse (key word) as to why I was not qualified.

- "There is dust in that corner that has to be cleaned right away or I won't sleep tonight."

- "I am groggy from my nap. I may not be able to learn what I need to know."

- "My big toe hurts, I won't be able to hike."

- "I poked myself in the eye with my eyeliner pencil and will not have perfect vision."

Instead I jumped right in and was taught how to do it. I was taught how to keep my groups from falling in a crevasse or to stop a toupe from being blown off or teeth from blowing out in the rotor wind as the helicopter landed to take us on another adventure.

People followed me and caught my enthusiasm, even the grumpy ones who thought they needed to find a phone to call their office. Luckily phones were hard to find on top of a ridge overlooking a glacier and cell phones, just coming into being did not work there. Barriers came down and there was unlimited possibility. I watched many of my guests who had been hesitant to begin a new life or to decide yes or no to a business venture change and were willing to go for the adventure.

I was recently hiking and came across a few women who were resting from a big rock scramble. They were most friendly and it was a good place for a water break. As we chatted they said they were on the hike to really clear their minds of brain chatter and to try to follow their intuition. They were thinking of going into network marketing, one of my passions, but they came up with excuse after excuse why they could not begin just then. After chatting with the women, they decided to hike with me. It took no time at all for them to keep step, slow as they needed to, to observe their surroundings instead of complaining how hard the climb was. We laughed as we splashed through water found our way around the muddy bog and realized that our water proof boots were not water proof. We found excitement in the trees, bushes, even bugs. They saw their first deer. By the time we reached the top they were enthused about going into their business. Suddenly they were

Wonder Women, ready to conquer. Fear (key word) was no longer the reigning emotion.

The **KEY WORDS** I mentioned in the previous pages will be a turning point in your success.

EXCITEMENT:

It is nice to want to try something new but do you have the excitement to carry it out? Are you willing to channel that excitement into the time it will take to become a success? Is each new day a fun challenge as you begin to see the fruits of your time and effort blossom?

Excitement will get and hold your attention. I get excited when starting ventures. I get excited thinking about my next fun trip and the planning of it. I get excited knowing I have a fun weekend planned. Think about your last excitement. How did it feel?

If you can remember that time, the same feeling will come back. Use that feeling as you jump right in.

As a network marketer, I become excited about the product and that genuine feeling carries to the people who want to come on board with me, follow my lead, be willing to come into the adventure.

Enjoy the journey! Laugh!

If you feel the excitement beginning to wane…giggle. Don't take yourself so seriously.

I get the giggles all the time and sometimes when I do not feel like laughing or giggling, I smile and the excitement returns.

You are ready to take your adventure/business to the top. Focus on the excitement of possibilities!

PASSION:

This follows excitement. They go hand in hand. You need to have the passion to climb any hurdles to make your goals. Without the passion to sustain you, boredom sets it. What is the next goal to be achieved?

In hiking it may be the next hill or boulder to get around. In business it may be how to set up your internet reach. Once that is done you set your sights on the next goal. Your passion will grow as you see each piece of the puzzle fall into place.

Be the author and creator of the work you love. Give yourself permission to explore your passion. Follow your intuition. If you cannot find the job you built your major in college around or you found it but it is not rewarding you, what would happen if you created the job you love? If that is not totally for you, what if you created a job you love to do part time?

EXCUSES:

These are giant stumbling blocks when trying to begin a new job or to try something new and adventurous. Listen to yourself. How are you trying to rationalize why you cannot do it? Seriously…did you really get stuck in the checkout line at the store without your credit card and had to put everything back, then go home to find the card, only to discover it had expired and you had to get a new one?

"I will start a business" – did you do it?

"I will begin a world peace movement." – did you do it?

"I will save an endangered species" – did you do it?

"I will follow my passion" – did you do it?

Why not?

This leads to "What If?""What if" will drive you nuts and possibly keep you in the safe zone of fear and excuses forever.

- What if I fail?
- What if no one agrees with me?
- What if I cannot have others join me in the venture?
- What if it costs money I do not think I have?
- What if I need to mow the grass before I begin?
- What if I cannot handle the traffic if I get it?
- What if I am always busy so finding the time to do it is impossible?

- What if I absolutely need to watch that TV show?
- What if I need to text my friend?
- What if I succeed?

I am exhausted just reading the "what ifs". It makes me want to take a nap. We could "what if" our way out of every new adventure. There is no sure way to know if you can do it unless you try!

Remember when you had a 2-year old or were around one? Everything you say is followed by "Why" from the child and finally you give up trying to answer and say, "Because I said so." As an adult "What if" replaces the "why?" of the child.

Stop right now and listen to yourself. How many "what ifs" and excuses do you come up with in a day? Jot them down. Are they really valid or could you have put them aside to accomplish at least one goal in that day? Could you have called a few people who would be interested in your new business? Could you have taken the time to decide and implement your next move?

It is so easy to get caught up with the negative possibilities that we talk ourselves out of our initial drive to start something new! I have been there. It was not until I really listened to myself try to **What If** my way out of something that I saw what I was doing and reversed the thoughts as soon as they came.

Avoid the fixation on failure. This makes you buy into what the people at the beginning of this chapter were trying to get you to believe in the first place. Besides, you have already distanced yourself from these people. Be willing to say who you are and what you do with confidence.

Find the value in your business and tout it to the world.

I could have been stopped by fear of the "What If's" but instead I chose to find the path to succeed. Look at the other side of fear. There are endless possibilities of things going magnificently or turning into something exciting that you never expected! Do not miss out on the possibilities of what might be. If necessary, look in the mirror and say, "yes I can!" Now, say it with conviction.

FEAR-

This word alone could become the queen of emotions if you let it as you begin the path to success. In network marketing, I need to realize that not everyone will say "yes" and to take the "no's" for a "no" and move on. I could let the fear of never being able to get someone to join my team rule the day, cause me to want to quit or drive me into a feeling of defeat. Nobody wants that. I look at it as another mountain to conquer.

In looking at fear, we have it for a reason. Our ancestors used it for flight or fight to survive. Examine what your fear is. Maybe it is asking you to step back, analyze your options so that you take a positive step forward. Pace yourself. You do not always have to rush in with a rash decision nor do you need to remain paralyzed. This only allows someone else to take your idea and run with it. That can lead to a whole other mess of emotions we are not getting into here.

What is your fear? Give it a name like Dragonguts, Ghostpoo, or Whackit. As soon as you do that it suddenly sounds ludicrous and it loses its punch. It is only a name that is slowing you down and your mind gave it life. Now it is just a piece of tissue paper to toss away. Remember the giggles? Toss it with humor.

Learn all the ins and outs of your new adventure. If it is network marketing, learn about the product. If it is creating a product, research what is out there and the need for it. Become familiar with all the ins and outs. Suddenly you are an expert and there is no room for fear to creep in.

Try a mental map of your success, not the fear. What is your outcome goal? Do you want to drive a fancy sports car? Can you see yourself in the house in the country with your two Golden Retrievers, wide open space and your company running as smooth as pie? Or do you want that Penthouse apartment?

When I was in theater, we would rehearse every night as a group and when I was alone I would go over my lines and how I wanted my character to be portrayed. We did not just get a script and do the show for the audience without preparation and constant visualization on how the show would come out. If we did not like something, we changed it. So go over and over in your head how you will be a success, what your outcome will be and the steps to get there. Practice what you want to say in front of the mirror.

How big is that fear anyway? It is not tangible. It is something you are creating in your head. I bet that fear in there is worse than anything that is really happening.

You may take a stumble here and there but I bet you fell down many times when you were taking your first baby steps. You tried different ways such as grabbing a stool, doing a downward dog yoga position ending in a somersault, using daddy's pant leg. You were creative and did not keep trying the same method which did not work the first time. Keep trying and do not let the fear of falling down stop you. Pivot and look in another direction. There are people out there who are willing to help you be a success. Let them be your footstool or pant leg and get on up there!

Have a positive attitude. This goes back to giggling, my favorite way to enjoy all of my adventures. I live in New York City. This can be irritating at times with cars honking, people pushing and dog poo to step around. Can I giggle my way out of the negative mood this can cause? You bet! I am not going to step in the dog poo but around it. I will find the humor in an ordinary situation. I will not let the dog poo in the minds of those wishing to distress me bring me down. Find the humor in it and with a positive attitude, you will succeed.

I love using the analogy of my hiking because I have found it parallels all my real world endeavors. I cannot look at anything in nature without seeing the positive.

Focus on the adventure, not the problems. Give yourself permission to explore.

Starting something new is something to put your passion into, not the fears and what ifs. It is another adventure in your life and can be rewarding, exciting and interesting. Think of all the new things you will learn.

The top is still there but the journey may not follow the exact course initially laid out. Pivot, have a sense of humor, be an adventurer, giggle, beat to the tune of your own drummer and be the success, not the naysayer.

> "Afoot and light-hearted I take to the open
>
> road,
>
> Healthy, free, the world before me,
>
> The long brown path before me leading
>
> wherever I choose."
>
> Walt Whitman "Song of the Open Road"

***

To contact Missy:

RadientAdventures.com

missygrohne@gmail.com

Instagram – melissa.grohne

Facebook – Missy's Adventures

Roxanne Tuomela

Thirty years ago, after experiencing multiple deaths in her family, Roxanne was on a quest to live her happiest, healthiest life. She invested in herself by becoming a board-certified, holistic health coach and a member of the AADP. Her education and entrepreneurial spirit gave her courage to start her own business working with men, woman and children, ages 7 to 77.

Taking things a step further in her own transformation, Roxanne became certified as a master in TCM. She opened NHL Health Coach working with athletes one-on-one and with teams in group programs. Roxanne wrote the award-winning book *The Puck Stops Here ~ Healthy Eating Handbook for Hockey Players*.

Roxanne didn't stop there with her desire to help others. Her most recently published book *The Belief Challenge* shares with the reader her proven method on how manifest through God anything, anyone, and any experience into one's life. She works with others one-on-one teaching them how to connect with their God and angels.

New ideas flow effortlessly to her when spent outdoors with her family boating, hunting and fishing. Stay tuned! Inevitably, Roxanne will be introducing something new to help others live their happiest, healthiest life.

Improving Lives via Courage, Action, Connection and Commitment

by Roxanne Tuomela

Hello, my creative one! Let me start off by saying, "You are NOT crazy!" In fact, your idea is brilliant! You have come up with a solution to improve the lives of others. You have something everyone wants and *needs*. Think about how your idea is going to make the world a better place. Isn't that exciting! You will be responsible for positively affecting everyone you know and even those you don't. Your client's/consumer's life will become richer because of you and your unique idea.

Now, stop for a moment, and ask yourself, "What if I don't follow through with my dream, what will happen then?" Do you have the courage it takes to make it all happen? Think of it this way, if you do not take a leap of faith and invest in your product/service, who will miss out? *Everyone* and that includes you.

Okay. Now, quickly, switch gears. Flip the switch back to the positive. Imagine a world where your product/service is helping others. It's bringing joy, happiness and freedom to the consumer. It is providing a solution to one's problem. Picture, for a moment, your own business, your invention, your vision has come to life and it's flourishing and you have become a member of the elite "2% club". You are now known as a successful entrepreneur. You are wealthy, wealthier than you ever imagined. What will that do for you, for your loved ones? How will you spend your millions? More importantly, how will you share your wealth with others? Are you ready to become a member? A member of the rich code club! A club of visionaries, a tribe of entrepreneurs who think outside of the box. Do you see what a difference you can make? You must allow yourself to dream, and dream BIG!

My grandparents were dreamers. Neither were high school graduates, yet, together, they turned their dreams into reality. They found the courage to do what others thought they couldn't do. They pushed aside the naysayers, and stepped into their faith by asking for guidance from their God to help them become successful businesses owners.

My grandfather put his blood, sweat and tears into his own commercial fishing business, on Lake Superior, and my grandmother put her whole heart and soul into opening up a restaurant, in their town of Marquette. As a result, their success allowed them to be their own boss (every entrepreneur's goal), provide for their family, be of support to friends, offer a hand to a stranger in need. The bonus was to afford a lifestyle free from financial worries. Their silver lining was leaving behind a legacy that no one thought possible from two young adults.

My entrepreneurial ancestors found the courage to take action upon their ideas, connect with God and made a commitment to serve others through their fruits of their labor. For decades, these two beautiful souls nourished the lives of their family, friends and neighbors. Wouldn't you love to do the same?

Just remember, you can be an entrepreneur at any age and stage of your life. And, if you've been told you can only do things one way, don't succumb to another's belief. Let me ask you, "What are you afraid of? What would happen if you failed? Or what would happen if you were to succeed?" My mentors taught me that fear is not tangible, it is simply a thought. In order to move forward, you must dive deep into your thoughts and feelings. Most importantly, you must work through your fears and push them aside once and for all. Believe in yourself and follow your heart.

Now that we have found your courage. It is time to take action! It's all going to take time and money. Don't think you know it all. You must be open and willing to learn from others and that doesn't necessarily mean you have to be in a classroom environment. You should seek out a mentor or mentors. My grandparents didn't have any mentors, but God sent them the earth angels they needed. You will need to seek out investors. Who do you know that would be willing to invest in your dream? Again, if no one comes to mind, don't worry they will appear if you have faith. Surround yourself with individuals who believe in you. Find a tribe that will support you every step of the way. You must trust in yourself to recognize when earth angels fall into your lap, individuals who stretch you beyond your comfort zone. Always follow your gut instincts whether you have warm and fuzzy goosebumps or if you're experiencing a chill down the spine. Pay attention to how you are feeling. Bottom line, do what is best for *you.*

To take further action you will need to consider your brand. Have you worked with a brand manager? What is your brand? How did you come up with your brand? The best advice I can offer you is to be authentic. Try to not let others steer you away from who you really are. It helps to think about brands you are familiar; which ones do you love and admire? It's also good to be aware of which brands make you feel squeamish? Pay close attention to how things make you *feel*? How will your potential clients *feel* about your brand?

No matter where you are in your life's journey, it is my intention to help you with your next chapter. I wish to be "the influencer". I want to inspire you and create great enthusiasm so that you are running with your hair on FIRE! I wish to cause excitement to course through your veins so that you will take action to get your idea/product/service out to the public so that you can serve and help others.

Right now, all I want is for you to not wait another day to take action. Do anything, do something! Take one small step toward your goal. Write up a business plan. Reach out to someone you would love to be your mentor. Hire a brand manager. Just do something to get the wheels turning. And, *then*, hold on tight because this is going to be like a runaway locomotive! Once you get going, trust that you will be unstoppable.

Congratulations on finding the fire in one's belly to put things into motion. "How does that *feel*? Are you *really* ready for this all to happen?" Yes, yes, of course, you are!

This now leads to your connections. What *connection* may you be missing? This is where cracking the rich code comes in. Are you ready for me give you the secret to cracking the rich code? What is the secret? It is God, God and His angels. Are you aware that He has assigned a group of heavenly and earth angels specifically for *you?* Through God you can manifest your dream, turn your idea into reality. You must ask God to please send you angels to assist you with your project. This may sound a bit "woo-woo," but it's not. God wants *you* to be successful. God has a bountiful life planned for *you*. He has enough abundance to spread about for *everyone*. There is proof. Let's start from the beginning . . .

Each and everyone one of us came into this world as a beautiful miracle and we all had to learn to crawl, walk and then run. You may have taken your first steps with help from your mom or dad or, perhaps, you took them all alone. It does not matter, either way you did it! Well, nothing has changed since you were a toddler. You had the courage to take action then and you have it now. However, as an adult, you need not go it alone. Take notice of the angels around you, heavenly angels God has placed in your life. Your earth angels are simply waiting with bated breath for you to ask for help. Taking your first steps was quite the victory. Now, is the time to experience the thrill of the birth your invention/idea/product/service. Imagine the joy, the celebration that awaits you.

The question remains, how did others go from waddling toddler to *blessed* beyond words? Take, for instance, Oprah. She started out worse than most of us, in a poverty-stricken environment, though through her own connection with her God, her life turned around. Oprah wanted to help others share their story and she did. She created a multi-*billion*-dollar media empire and she is said to be one of the most influential women in the world. She has positively touched the lives of millions. You can do the same.

I know you have seen many award shows celebrating actors, musicians and athletes. Have you noticed that each and every one of them looks up to the sky and points a finger and they say, "Thank you. Thank you, God." These individuals all started out just like you and me, from womb to crawling, to walking and then sprinting. It is safe to assume they found the courage to take action through God, they developed an unbreakable connection to God and they made a commitment to be their best and utilize their God-given talents. That is the truth of the matter. Do you know what your own unique talents are? If you don't, not to worry, your angels will point them out for you. That being said, it is time to start utilizing your gifts.

So, what are you waiting for? God is waiting to hear from you. It is up to you to reach out and connect with your God. Start your conversations with God every morning. Thank God for the abundance you have already received. Gratitude is key. Tell God you are ready. God will arrange for the universe to bring to you everything you need.

When I became ready, I asked to receive signs from God and my angels. Sure as a whirl I began noticing individuals appearing in my life; they were God sent. With my faith and trust in God I willingly invested in programs for myself, and I will forever cherish all that I have learned from mentors. My dreams started to become reality.

I upped the ante and found ways to heighten my connection with God. I started to put together, what I call, a "manifestation station™". Things started to happen for me more rapidly and with clarity when I started to create my manifestation stations™. I picked a sacred place in my home and placed a candle, angel figurines and other objects that symbolized what it was that I was wishing to manifest through God.

Every morning, I light my candle, open my journal and I reach out to God in writing asking for some direction of where I may be of service. I ask God to send me individuals whom I can help, individuals I can show the way on how to live their happiest, healthiest life.

I asked God to provide me the vehicle which would help me reach millions of people, and here I am. God sent me my own earth angels, Jim Britt, Kevin Harrington and Joel Sauceda. I received the opportunity to become a co-author, to write a chapter in this book, a chance to teach others on how to become rich in all areas of life and to share my proven methods on how to become a successful entrepreneur. This is a perfect example of joining an amazing tribe, in my case, a tribe of authors longing to improve lives by sharing their experiences, their knowledge and methods only to witness the birth of another breathtaking idea/product/service/invention, to be a part of the creation of another millionaire.

Please create your own manifestation station™. Find a special place in your home or office to place a candle, an angel figurine and other objects which represent what it is that you are wishing to manifest into your life. Purchase a special journal for yourself and write daily thanking your God and angels for all of your blessings and for all of the good that is coming from your success as an entrepreneur. Express gratitude for the blessings others will receive because of you and your vision.

Courage, action, connection . . . what's next? Commitment. Kind of like the three little pigs. Who was the most committed piggy to sticking around, the pig with the most solid foundation. Forget going in lightly. You must be solid as a brick to your conviction of becoming a multi-millionaire. And, in order to do so, you will need to create a solid foundation which to build your business.

To help yourself build upon your foundation you will need to understand, your "why"? Ask yourself, "Why is what I do important to me? How does this differentiate me from others? What drives me?" Define your purpose, your "why". What excites you? And why? What do you FEEL? What do you get out of it? Who or what is your priority? What is the legacy you wish to leave behind? All of this is critical to creating the business and life that you desire.

At this stage of the game you will need to make a commitment to yourself and your values. What are your core values? Here are some examples of just a few core values that come to mind: faith, integrity, authenticity, loyalty, honesty, responsibility, respect, innovation, being of service to others, being committed to doing the right thing, living a life in balance, having a sense of humor, being humble, being socially responsible, allowing yourself the freedom of self-expression, being open-minded and kind-hearted.

Write down your core values and post them where you can see them each and every day. Put your list of values in your manifestation station™.

Create a mission statement. A mission statement is the "how" and "what" you do to achieve your goals and always remaining true to your core values.

Here is my mission statement: Through God, I will fulfill my purpose by helping others connect with their God and their angels so they may live a life rich in faith, love, joy, health and wealth.

My most powerful core value is believing God wants the best for each and every one of us.

To stand in my truth, to be authentically me. That is one of my core values.

Another core value of mine is to not judge others. I have taught my children, "Everyone has their own idea of a good time"; words of wisdom I learned from my Grandmother. If you live by these words, you'll find yourself never judging another. Try it, it works.

I am grateful that my family and friends believe in me and my dreams. I am blessed to be authentically me when I am with my family and friends and to have the strength to be true to myself with strangers. I thank my family and friends for never judging me for some of the choices I have made.

Do you have this same kind of support? If not, take a close look around you and ask yourself if the friends and family you surround yourself with are helping you or if they are getting in the way of your dreams; are they interfering with your core values? It is imperative that you cut loose those who are hindering your success and interrupting your connection with God and your angels.

Living my life believing in God, standing in my truth and not judging others allows me to live by my mission statement.

To sum things up: 1) You need to find your courage. Don't be afraid to make changes and take a chance. It is called *bravery*. Do you have the courage to become a successful entrepreneur; 2) You must take action and invest in yourself and your invention/idea/product/service because nothing will get done unless you do; 3) You need to find your deepest place in faith and connect with your God and ask for your angels to step forward to help you; 4) Commit and never give up until you reach your goal(s).

I know you can appreciate that this is only the beginning. As successful entrepreneurs we thrive on the next BIG idea/invention/product/service. Our creative juices will never stop flowing and what a blessing that is!

Yes, I'm currently working on another idea. Please stay tuned. And, remember, courage, action, connection and commitment! With love, Roxanne

***

To contact Roxanne:

Email: author.roxannetuomela@gmail.com
Website: https://www.roxannetuomela.com
Facebook: https://www.facebook.com/roxannetuomela/
Instagram: https://www.instagram.com/roxannetuomela/
Twitter: https://twitter.com/RoxanneTuomela
LinkedIn: https://www.linkedin.com/in/roxanne-tuomela-066b4132/

Karl Roller

Mr. Roller's respected International Entrepreneurial reputation spans decades.

Early on, paper routes, mowing lawns, and giving guitar lessons provided cash-flow for the young Mr. Business-man. By age 24, as General Building Contractor, his resume' eventually show-cased 52 multi-million-dollar custom built homes in Southern California.

Shifting business gears, the International Network Marketing Industry drew him in to appreciate a successful 35-year career!

Wearing executive hats as company owner, president and CEO of other companies also a company owner providing nutritional and skin care products at wholesale to the Network Marketing Industry. One of few networkers in the Industry successfully building and maintaining multiple business organizations simultaneously.

As a record Producer (Music), one particular cut was used to awaken astronauts on the last two shuttle missions. Also producing thousands of CD's and DVD's promoting and communicating his method of business training.

His business acumen and talent awarded him both the "Telly Award" and an "International Communications Award".

A talented speaker and presenter, gifted with the ability to deliver his brand of business training and tools professionally and heart-driven. His greatest joy is inspiring people to invest in their own personal development, creating successful business leaders.

Is That My Chair?

By Karl Roller

You might be wondering about the title of this chapter, ***"Is That My Chair?"*** The reason I chose that title is because oftentimes today we find ourselves in a position where we may wonder *if* we *deserve* to be where we are? Perhaps we're actually in a position of authority, influence or power and we don't even *feel* like we deserve it. It's kind of like looking at a *chair* and saying *"that belongs to someone that has a certain personality trait, power or influence."* Thinking to yourself, *"I don't belong in that chair"* when in fact; you do. Or, maybe you find yourself in a *chair* in a position of influence and you might not think you deserve to be there because you didn't work hard enough, long enough, etc.

Do you feel that maybe some *fairy dust* landed on you which is the only reason you are successful or have accomplished what you have? Not to undervalue *fairy dust* but I can tell you we (all of us that have achieved anything of value) can all say some has landed on us.

I remember once reading that Richard Branson was asked if he felt he was lucky? His response to that question was *"Of course I feel lucky. I was born in a first world country, everyone born in a first world country is lucky!"*

So, sometimes when we've accomplished a lot and we've become a person of influence we may have had a degree of *success* in our life and as a result of that *success*, we consider ourselves *lucky*, and that may be the *only* reason we feel that we are in the position we're in, whatever that position is.

But the reality is we're in *that* position because we're not *just lucky*, because *lucky* is something that we all experience. I think anyone who's really accomplished anything of merit and value has to look back on that *stroke of luck* and see its role in our *success*. Oftentimes we were working on a project and found significant areas in which *luck* played a part.

I know from my own personal experience, I've had a lot of *lucky breaks*, if you will. I had certain ventures that came into my life at *just the right time* and I said *just the right thing at just the right moment*, you might say and I may have looked at it as being *lucky*. But the reality is, even if I had that *so-called luck* and had the right mentorship etc., if I hadn't taken *action;* if I'd hesitated on pulling that trigger, then the *luck* would not have been manifested in specific results. I wouldn't be able to look back on what I consider now to have been *luck,* if I hadn't taken advantage of the opportunities as they arose. Recognizing when *luck or happenstance* actually happens and doing something about it are two very different things.

Most people have events that could have made a huge difference in *how* their life worked out and for one reason or another they chose *not* to pull that trigger of action which makes all the rest look easy. If you're a *"trigger puller"* you take the *luck* out of it.

So, if you find yourself possibly feeling a little *uncomfortable* in *getting comfortable,* it's okay because it's quite *deserved.* You may even consider yourself great and perhaps it's not something that you would admit to or share with others, but you think *"hey, what I did is really great!"* and finding yourself in that position there's a few things that you need to do. Treat the influence that you now have with great respect and learn how to find out *how you created it, how to use it,* and *how to invest it.*

One of the things that you can do which will speed up the process is to find a *mentor.* Many of you have already found them; I do recommend more than one. You probably have had at least one mentor and that's why you were able to accomplish what you have already accomplished. But you may need to change. Upgrade your mentorship! You may need to upgrade your mentor because as you mature in your business ability, as well as grow socially, personally and spiritually you may need to find someone who does or knows what you want to know about or feel inspired to want to do next. Or, find that mentor to teach you something that *you don't know that you don't know.* Enlist their help to take you to the next level. *That* learned experience truly is the difference in many cases between being somebody who has influence on a small number of people versus someone who has influence over a great number of people, the difference being between a $100,000 earner or a *Million Dollar Earner.* Art Williams once said, *"The difference between a $50,000 a year earner and a $500,000 a year executive is that the $500,000 a year executive believes a little bit more, tries a little bit more, cares a little bit more, stays up a little bit more, calls a little bit more, sponsors a little bit more, loves a little bit more. Just do it. Winners do it until it's done!"*

Remember that influence is the currency of leadership!

Also, you'll have to learn to *accept* your greatness, not in an egotistical way, but in an authentic and real way, a humble way and a modest way. It can be done, and when you *DO* accept it, then you can *expect* greatness, you can *respect* greatness, you can *protect* greatness. You can actually develop a *passion* for greatness and somehow you then *get access* to even more greatness!

If you're building a team you *must remember* that whatever *kind* of individual you're trying to recruit or develop; *you must be* yourself. Jim Rohn once said, *"If you want to be a leader who attracts quality people, the key is to become a quality person yourself."* So, if you want *honest* people, *you* have to *be honest,* a *dishonest* person *cannot* recruit an *honest* person. If you want *productive* people, you must be *productive.* If you want *energetic* people you must be *energetic* if you want *positive* people you must be *positive.* To put it another way *"A" players* want to play with other *"A" players.* If an *"A" player* is surrounded by *"B" players* the *"A" player* will *become* a *"B" player.* An interesting phenomenon is, if an *"A" player is attracting other "A" players* and the team becomes a team of *"A" players* they become more and more *attractive* to other players and the quality of the overall team *rises* very quickly because everyone *wants* to be on their team! It's really a measurement of your leadership skills.

And, of course you *must* lead by example. When you're in a leadership role you're *always* leading, whether good or bad, you're *always* leading. You want to lead by *example* and judge by *results.* You have probably heard this before but it could not be more true than when you're building an organization and working with a team.

You seem to be in *that chair* we call *Success.* We have to make sure that everyone around us is there for the right reasons. Steve Jobs once said, *"When I hire someone really senior, competence is the ante. They have to be really smart but the real issue for me is, are they going to fall in love with Apple because if they fall in love with Apple, everything else takes care of itself."* So many times when we are in a recruiting phase we think that we need to find other reasons to bring them into our endeavor. The reality is, if they don't *love* what we're doing regardless of our leadership skills they're not going to *stay* long, they're not going to be a *part* of the team for long. They really have to *love* not only our leadership but also what we are *about* and what we're *doing.* If you find yourself in a leadership role and you're *not* getting the results you're looking for; *not* making the money that you want, it's because there may be some lessons you have *yet* to learn. Or, you too, may have fallen victim to getting involved for the *wrong reasons* and may need to *reset* your core values and *do a check* on your *alignment;* product, company, team and mission of the endeavor. It could also be the *culture* of the company/project that you're *not* in *alignment* with.

You may find yourself trying to build a new venture and needing course corrections. This is normal. In football, this is the reason for *half-time.* Consider a good team which has usually won the game with ease against an old team; Alas, the old team now has a new *new* coach. Hence, it's a different game altogether. *Half-time* gives the coach and team an *opportunity* to re-evaluate all the *tactics*, all the *strategy* being put forth, all the *team players* which are in place and all the *preconceived ideas* and set them aside. Time for a *new* set of ideas and initiatives to implement in order to accomplish the goal of *winning the game!*

Many times we find ourselves in *that chair of success* and we've *stopped* doing the things that got us into *that chair* because we think we have *arrived* and we no longer *need* to continue the efforts which proved to be so successful in our journey. We began to take our position for granted and thus developed a *feeling of entitlement* which is a *cancer* in any organization. It may be time for us to *reboot, reconnect* and start *reminding* ourselves of *all* the things that we used to do that were so successful, which we *stopped* doing because we thought we *had it down* and *had it done*. Remember, you are *always leading* and if you fall back into the thought process of *entitlement,* your team will do the same and then *disaster* will follow.

If you are preparing to run a marathon and you have never run a marathon before, you would have to do a lot of work in order to be prepared to run in the marathon. However, once you've done all the training and the hard work in order to *qualify* to actually run in that marathon, possibly resulting in a *win,* would you then *stop* your training and feel since you have done it once that now you're set with nothing more to ever do? And when the next marathon comes would you have a *chance* to win again if you *stopped* doing all the things that you did in order to *qualify* to be in the first marathon? Of course not! You realize right away that if you are going to be one that *runs* marathons, it is an *ongoing* discipline that has to be *maintained* in order for you to be *relevant* in the next contest. It is the same thing with anything we try to do in business or even personally and spiritually. It's not something you can do one time and you're set for life. This is an *ongoing* endeavor which has to be maintained, that's why we call it a discipline because we have to be disciplined in order to *achieve it and maintain it.*

One of the ways that can make it a little easier for us is to *focus*. To be successful in this kind of work, it is important to be very clear about what we're *trying to accomplish*; have clear instructions and expectations. We *must* be *responsible and believable* in order to create motivation as a result. *Believability* is so important! If the goal is not truly believable we lose *credibility* with ourselves and we will *lose* before we *begin*. I can't overestimate the *power of full engagement* and there are four key areas of *engagement*. The 4 areas or dimensions of *engagement* that I'm talking about are:

1. *Physical.* Which means you've got to be *energized, physically energized* in order to *accomplish* these goals.

2. *Emotional.* That means you've got to be *connected, engaged,* looking for an *emotional response* or *connection.* Looking for the *feeling* that goes along with *accomplishment.*

3. *Mental.* You've got to be *focused,* it takes real *focus* to *accomplish* what needs to be done with a new endeavor, trying to *keep* your team *in place and active.*

4. *Spiritual.* Your spirituality *has* to be *in line* or *aligned* with your stated goals. These four attributes *need* to be *balanced* in order for you to truly *be successful.*

Your *energy* can be *diminished* from being *overused* or *underused.* Recovery and balancing of stresses will be a key trait in finding your overall balance. *Stress* causes *burnout, breakdown* and *trauma.* Recovery will *require* the time needed to *re-energize.* Information from great sources and people, *seminars* and *support venues* which will help to *shore* up energy on the key four levels mentioned above. It *can* and *will* make *all* the *difference* in your being able to *maintain* your level of growth over time.

Don't be afraid to *ask more* of yourself and of others. You can do it. The stakes in self-discipline are high and *requires* getting rid of negative habits, *removing* barriers and *establishing* strategic positive energy *rituals.*

1. Define your purpose.

2. Face the truth.

3. Take action.

Here are a few things to *remember*. *Professionals* get paid for what they *know*. *Entrepreneurs* get paid for what they *DO* with what they *know*. Personal development is *part* of the process. It takes time to make the changes *needed* for any growth. Give yourself the time; you're trying to change your *consciousness*. The first *cause* of any positive result or negative result is always found within the thought process. If you're not having enough success it is due to your way of thinking; *always!*

Sometimes our past gets in our way. Remember, your past does *not* determine your future. In order for things to change for you, *you have to change!* It is as simple as that. If you don't have people following you it is because you're *not* leading! There's *something* you're missing. You need to *re-evaluate*, look at the fundamentals. Are you delivering the basics? Focus on your strengths. Here are a few things to check.

1. How much time do you spend *worrying* about finances?

2. How often are you *late* for appointments?

3. Do you ever *not do* what you say?

4. What was the last book you read, seminar you attended to *improve* on your stated goals?

5. How much time do you *allocate* for personal development?

6. Are you *envious* of those who *excel* around you?

7. Do you *learn* something of value from your mistakes?

8. By what rule do you *decide* what is good for you?

9. Do you *change* your mind often?

10. Do you *finish* what you start?

I've given you a lot of things to think about in this chapter. I hope that you've found some insight and ideas and maybe some things that you can implement.

One thing I *can assure* you of; when you put in the *time* and the *effort*, the *results* will be there. It's a formula that *always* works! If you *don't* find yourself in a position of success now or if you, as I mentioned in the title of this chapter, *"Is That My Chair?"* are questioning whether or not you *belong* in *the chair*, should you *strive* to be *in the chair* or maybe you're *already in the chair*, wondering if you *deserve to be* there or what it will take to *continue to be* there? In each and every one of these situations the answer is *always* the same; it's *maintaining* the direction we've talked about here, which is *putting* some basic fundamental *things* in place to make sure that we have *good habits* which will give us the *results* we're looking for.

It's *easier* than it seems, although there is work involved, it's not work that can't be done by any of us and all of us. It is in fact, our *duty* to *do* all we can to *be* all that we *are* and all that we *can be!* To do any less is *irresponsible* on our part. I remember once when I was at a training seminar in Palm Springs listening to Jim Rohn who was the key note trainer. I'll never forget the illustration that he used to demonstrate this idea to those of us there in the room that day.

He said, *"We are the only creation on the planet today that doesn't automatically do its best. How tall will a tree grow? It will send its roots out as far as it can. It's branches, out as far as they can, to get all the sun, all the moisture that it possibly can from all of its efforts, to grow as tall as it can. How tall will grass grow? As tall as it can! You've never seen grass that grew half as tall as it can. How far will a bird fly? As far as it can! In some cases, it will fly half way around the world to reach its destination. We, as mankind have been given the dignity of choice. Most of us choose not to do the best we can."*

So, the real *challenge* is, *can* we do the best we can, *should* we do the best we can? I believe that's why we're here. I *accepted* the challenge that he laid down that day, so I now *extend* that challenge to you. To *be the best* that you can be, to *reach out* as far as you can reach, *spread* your wings as far as you can spread them, and as far as they can reach. *Look up* and *soak* as much sunlight as you can, *taking all the fresh air* that your lungs can hold, *stretch* your arms out as high as they can stretch, your hands as open as they can be. *Receive all that you can receive.* You *deserve* it!

***

To contact Karl:

Email: karlroller@gmail.com

Phone: 760-421-4902

Twitter: karlroller

Linkedin: Karl Roller

Yvonne Oswald PhD,

Yvonne Oswald PhD, recognized global leader of Human Empowerment and award winning, best-selling author of *Every Word has Power*, now in eleven languages, is at the leading edge of the new field of Human Behavioral Technology. She is a renowned and respected International Keynote Speaker, Communications Trainer, Master Trainer of NLP, and Master Trainer of Hypnosis. U.S. National Awards include; **Most Unique Contribution to the Field of Clinical Hypnosis** for her unique techniques in changing negative self-talk and DNA Transformation, and the **COVR Visionary Award nomination for 'Mind Magic'**, her pioneering process of clearing a negative emotion in less than a minute. Her work with war vets, PTSD and depression is outstanding. Dr. Yvonne's unparalleled 4-hour Breakthrough Blueprint is a remarkable innovation in the field of Neurological Medicine. She has an outstanding reputation for her exciting, innovative, fun, and interactive trainings in both public and private sectors.

A British born, certified teacher with 20+ years' experience, Dr. Yvonne clears challenges for every audience (Internet, live, radio, and television) and assists others to go beyond their boundaries to reach the success they desire. Her You Tube channel is available worldwide.

Wealthy Mind Equals Wealthy Wallet

Success from the Inside Out!

By Yvonne Oswald PhD

Health and Wellness Industry Entrepreneurship

People often say to me, "You're so lucky to be an entrepreneur, self-employed and successful – you can take time off whenever you want and organize your own schedule for a vacation." What time off? What vacation? Oh! Do you mean the fifteen hour days and the sleepless nights wondering how the mortgage is going to get paid every month? People don't realize how much time and energy goes into making entrepreneurship an overnight success story! The word entrepreneur actually means risk taker, but there's a big difference between speculation and a sure opportunity!

It's new! It's different! But will it sell? When you have your amazing solution that's going to change the world, be aware that if it's not already out there, people probably aren't going to buy it if they don't immediately recognize its value. The key here to fast progress is modeling someone who has already proven results rather than starting a whole new idea that may not catch on for years. NLP (Neuro Linguistic Programming) is based on the idea of modeling excellence and making it replicable. It's better to have a high probability product or service to achieve fast and sustainable success. A good pilot test upfront will save you so much time and money down the line. When you have an established track record, it's so much easier to introduce your new concepts. And THEN you can really change the world!

After university in England and gaining my teaching degree, I moved to South Africa where I lived for four years until I was 25, working as head of human resources for the Bantu Administration (I learned to speak Zulu). I then went on to teach English as a Second Language in Rome, Italy for three years (I learned Italian) and sold Real Estate in Portugal for the following two years. I returned to England and, along with substitute teaching, began facilitating meditation and healing classes from my home. After traveling and tasting the good life, I was eager to explore and travel more, so I immigrated to Toronto, Canada, in my mid-thirties. I started taking workshops to address the abuse I had experienced as a child. My father was sexually, physically and verbally abusive, so I signed up for every emotional workshop possible to help me address the issues. I learned about physical cleansing, gestalt therapy, talk therapy, massage, rebirthing, reiki and every other therapy possible to balance me in every way. I needed to make a living too, so I studied courses that enabled me to work with and teach others. I tried my hand at Network Marketing but quickly realized it wasn't for me because most successful Network Marketers made it their full-time career.

I eventually discovered hypnosis and realized that this was the one modality that worked sweetly and easily when everything else had just put a lid on negative events without clearing them. After encountering life changing NLP, that was that. I had found my calling.

I read everything I could get my hands on about starting my own business and then came across a marketing book that said, "If you're not an expert, read and learn everything you can to make you an expert, write a book about it and then *you* become the expert!" Now that I *could* do! As a lifelong learner, I'd been studying healing all my life, so I became a solopreneur. I qualified in Trainers' Hypnosis and NLP and completed my PhD in Clinical Hypnosis in nearly seven years, along with a late marriage and having a baby at 42. I wrote my book, 'Every Word has Power', about how to change and speak positively to yourself (85% of our self-talk is negative!) and it became a best seller in eleven languages. It was published by Beyond Words ('The Secret' publisher) and distributed by Simon and Schuster. Speaking and Teaching NLP worldwide, facilitating corporate, private and group sessions, became the norm.

Sounds great doesn't it? You have no idea how often I worked all night to complete a PhD paper, or how many days I spent making the two-hour presentation at Harvard Medical School sound 'spontaneous'! Success? Yes. More than I ever dreamed. So let me go ahead now and save you twenty years, by giving you success secrets in the health and wellness business that actually work. It's not enough to have a great business idea or product – you also need to know how to sell it and make money from it! Whether you're just starting out, or are already established, you may well find some of my ten minute tips extremely useful!

Entrepreneur Triangle

For an entrepreneur or solopreneur health and wellness coach, these three areas: Helping People, Money and Success / Fame / Recognition, are the entrepreneur requirements. The real challenge is that for years I was told that as long as I was passionate and helped people, then the money would come. It didn't work! I finally realized I had to make money a priority.

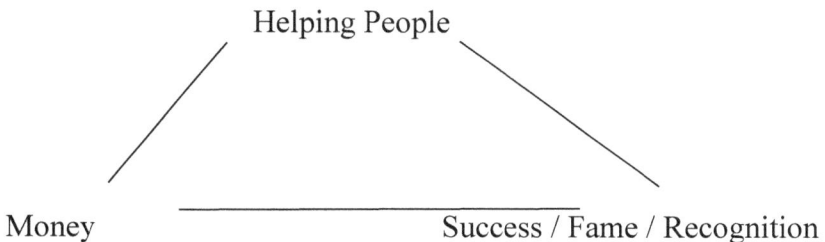

Helping People

Money   Success / Fame / Recognition

When asked to teach or speak, I started asking, "What's your budget for speakers?" A shocked reply: "We don't have a budget." Was followed by "What budget could you get together do you think?" It was amazing! Suddenly, not only was I getting real money for speaking, plus expenses, I was also getting more recognition and my online profile rose exponentially, resulting in more fame and more work so I was able to help that many *more* people! When planning a new idea or venture, make sure that your outlay for taking a training or buying a marketing plan/product can be recouped in six months or less to keep on top of the expenses involved. I know that when I teach a Hypnosis, Life Coach or NLP training I keep the price low so that my students can make their money back fast from client sessions and return to me for more training.

The brilliant thing about health and wellness right now is that it's a billion-dollar industry that requires no massive capital outlay or product once you've learned your craft. It's one of the most up and coming commercial enterprises to emerge this past twenty-years. Health and Wellness was finally acknowledged as being valuable in the corporate world with the realization that having healthy, mentally and emotionally well-adjusted people in the workforce boosts loyalty and productivity, vastly increasing the bottom line. And there are now so many options to choose from for specialization.

As far as alternative healthcare modalities go, Homeopathy, Chiropractic and Naturopathy are probably best set up in an office environment for insurance purposes, but certifications in Yoga, Meditation, Reiki, Reflexology, Rebirthing, Aromatherapy, Massage, Hypnosis, Therapeutic Touch, NLP, Life Coaching, Nutrition, Shiatzu and/or other complementary healthcare modalities can be practiced from your home office, or as part of a studio, spa, church, chiropractic office space or space rented on a part time basis. You're now on your way to being self-directed and having your own business!

Your first task is to reserve your domain name (e.g. GoDaddy.com). Domain names are real estate gold. Look up your potential site name on Amazon online (books) and Google to find out if it's in the correct genre. WiseOwl.com doesn't say much about what you do, so people may not find you easily! Actually, one of the best ways to get a domain is simply to use your own name because it doesn't restrict you to one area as you grow your business. Your website will never be 'finished', so first begin with one page (Wix.com or Squarespace.com) and add to it as you go! Improve it when you generate more income. Unless you're a web maven, Fiverr.com is excellent for finding capable people all over the world who can set your site up for a really great rate.

The front page of your site always has a tempting (free!) opt in call to action; a relaxation MP3 (Enlightened Audio sells royalty free music), a free ten page downloadable, Five Tips for …. Etc. with a link to a landing page. Have the landing page deliverable lead to the next step you want the prospect to take e.g. Book a consultation, or Buy a low cost ($7 to $37 product) which might lead to next higher priced offerings in your funnel. Clickfunnels.com is good for setting up your online funnel to market, sell and deliver your products and/or services.

Yes - your business card: Make sure you have your face on it!! At a convention with 300 or more people attending, the most important thing that others need to remember is who you are (and they don't like to throw a face away!). I used to go to conventions and come back with 60 cards. These days I aim to find just three good connections.

In the beginning, when I told people what I did and handed over my card: "I do hypnosis and NLP," people's faces would glaze and they'd back away! No one wants to believe or admit they need therapy! So, as you hand over your business card, simply state what you do and say, "I'm a Hypnosis Practitioner/Reiki Master/Massage Therapist" *(etc.)*. "If you have a friend who'd like a session could you give them my card please?" They usually respond with, "I've always wanted to do that! I might be interested myself. How much is a session?" You need to have your top price ready; simply state what you'd like to get. Their face will not change and they'll say great, or you'll notice a downfallen expression, at which point you say, "I'd actually like to work within your price range. How much were you thinking for a session?" When they name their price make sure you also have your bottom line price ready. Have your calendar right there in case they want to make an appointment; Acuity.com, or YouCanBookMe.com are great for online scheduling. For non-cash payments, PayPal and Square.com are easily set up for credit cards. 17hats.com is amazing for keeping online files, invoicing and sending receipts.

Instead of only giving your contact information, get theirs and tell them that you'll send them something for free – a ten page downloadable, an online MP3 to relax them, or a prosperity MP3. You can record a twenty minute MP3 with background music with Soundtrap.com or Garageband.com, or record it in a studio. I always give away my best MP3's – I want them to experience my work and come back for more.

Now you have your skill set and a basic model, it's time to build your list and get everyone to opt in. Around 5000 people for your newsletter is a good working number. Use block scheduling to create flow and ensure you're including all the functions of a business in your weekly routine:

a. Follow Up and Connection Calls

b. Content Creation time (for social media etc.)

c. Client Fulfilment time blocks

d. Administration

e. Networking, speaking engagements

Join a Mastermind Group, or start one. Commit to speaking to groups – anywhere and everywhere! Just be yourself in front of your clients. Make sure you simply pass around a sign in sheet (name, telephone and email) and give something away. I give two free online prosperity MP3's to get people's contact info. I tell them that I'll happily put them on my newsletter list to let them know about my future trainings/keynotes. I also let them know they can easily opt out.

Teach monthly classes from home. A monthly two-hour meditation class is easy to run and will build loyalty fast. Advertise it on Meetup.com or Eventbrite.com and then as they leave tell them to bring a friend next time. You'll get private clients from this. Make short 3-minute action and top tip videos for YouTube, livestream your top tips on Facebook or YouTube, conduct Teleseminars, do Tele summits with JV's, affiliates and promotional partnerships (just be careful of unexpected costs).

Having your own radio show can be expensive, time consuming and you usually promote someone else instead of yourself! Blog Talk Radio is free if you really want to go that route. I've found it much better to be a guest. Radio shows have 24/7 to fill, so having your 'Five tips for....' ready will get you any number of guest spots. Make yourself the expert. Find a special holiday/event date, then write your five tips article around it: http://www.holidayinsights.com/everyday.htm

Simply look up local or national radio shows, and send an email asking if they have a spot coming up for a guest. A blog will also get you opt-ins and it's a way to not only build your list, but also to sell advertising. A friend of mine has a mom's community blog and makes $15,000 a month from companies advertising products such as diapers, toys and baby food. Residual income is essential to see you through the ups and downs of entrepreneurship, so expand to an online sales store as soon as you can.

Social Media is important for getting you noticed. Take on one new social media platform per quarter to build your presence; build one successfully then move on to the next. Have a Facebook fun/personal/business page. Polish your LinkedIn profile to include your area of specialty and expertise. Pinterest, Instagram and Twitter can boost your fan base. Start your own free YouTube channel; this has been my best advertising tool of all. People watch my three minute videos, learn how to stop procrastination, clear negative emotions, goal set, clear phobias, then go straight to my website to book me for a private session or corporate engagement.

Once you're well established on the Internet, it's time to expand. At Health and Wellness expos, your clients are not the people attending – they're the ones who have the booths. Your job here is to make as many connections as possible and keynote and speak at as many conventions/women's groups/breakfast meetings imaginable. A training I attended in Las Vegas had fifteen top Fortune 500 decision makers explaining how they chose training and development instructors, or keynote speakers for conferences. In every case they simply asked someone they knew and trusted in their own company whom they could recommend.

Your Keynote Speech can be easily adapted to any engagement if you begin with a ten slide training slideshow. Create *one* great presentation for your first successful half-day workshop. Where do you begin? With a catchy, memorable title. Then....

Here's an outline of the sequence of the way the brain actually absorbs information that will make total sense of your slideshow presentation, talk, article or Keynote:

1. **WHY** is this important? I need reasons and relevance.

2. **WHAT** is it about (research, proof)? What are the facts? Analyze and make me think.

3. **HOW** do I make this happen? How does it work? Demonstrate. Can I have a go at making it work?

4. **WHAT IF**?...................................**Any questions?** What about....? What are the hidden possibilities? Evaluate and predict.

When pitching to corporate (or anyone else for that matter), it's very tempting to drone on about what you do, without taking into account what they actually need from you. We say in NLP that how you do one thing is how you do everything, so it's important to know the decision maker's buying strategy.

The ONLY question to ask is,

"So that I can help you better, let me just ask you: **What's most important**

to you about your ....X.... ? (health, home / business / property/ lifestyle / future)" "What else?" "What else?" Write their reply down *verbatim*.

1.

2.

3.

So for health I may want: 1. More energy 2. To stay slim 3. An easy health routine.

Your job is to repeat it back to them in EXACTLY the same order (1,2,3) that they gave it to you! "So that's interesting, because I have a wellness program that will give you more energy, make you stay slim and is an easy health routine. Are you interested in hearing more?" "Yes please!"

Go ahead and do this exercise with a friend; first in the right order, then read it backwards "I have another health program that will (3,2,1) Are you interested in hearing more?" You'll be amazed at how uninteresting the same words feel when given in a different order!

Finally, let me give you my seven tips for daily confidence boosting (before you sell or speak!):

1. **Power Center** - three fingers below your navel (Tan Dien). Imagine a powerful image there, a tiger, a puppy, or something that makes you smile. When you think of it, you'll automatically center and balance your energy.

2. **Belly breath** – take a deep breath that moves your diaphragm down and tells the unconscious mind that the danger is over.

3. **Tongue relaxed** - make sure your tongue is down at the bottom of your mouth – we hold it on the roof when we are stressed.

4. **Alpha state** – back straight, look up and chin up a little - become aware of 180 degrees peripheral vision. It's an amazing state that sends you into Alpha and relaaaaax.

5. **Set your Goals Small and Sweet** -Make one phone call - the rest will then be easy. Answer one e-mail - you'll have them all done in minutes. Go for one sale a day - you'll soon reach your target and easily surpass it. Take an hour for yourself every day.

6. **Drink plenty of fluids.** It boosts your brain and concentration ability by
   14% instantly.
7. **The CBA of success.** Conceive, Believe, Achieve

Set up great expectations with a long term goal and a short term hook.

Good luck and enjoy your new freedom. You were born to be different and to make a difference.

Shine your amazing light out to the world!
***

To contact Yvonne:

https://globalwelcome.com/

yvonne@globalwelcome.com

(416) 494 2233

https://www.facebook.com/yvonne.oswald.7

https://www.linkedin.com/in/yvonne-oswald-phd1234/

https://twitter.com/DrYvonneOswald

http://globalwelcome.com/free-cds/

Rylee Meek

Rylee Meek is the founder and CEO of the Social Dynamic Selling System, which turns dinner seminar marketing into a science. After responding to a small ad on Craigslist in 2009, Rylee was introduced to a new concept of selling, one in which radically changed his life forever. Having just $673 in his bank account, but more importantly a burning desire for more, Rylee went on to produce over $80 million in sales over the past 8 years. Now that he has perfected his model, through continual trial and error, he is sharing this learned wisdom, and is on a mission to help other entrepreneurs and business owners achieve the revenue goals they have to live the lifestyle they desire. Everything he teaches is tried, tested, refined, and proven to create a predictable, sustainable, and scalable selling system.

It's Not Just Dinner

By Rylee Meek

Who is Rylee Meek? How did I become the *Social Dynamic Selling* guy? As you know, Rylee is an uncommon name. I've had an uncommon journey.

It began in Miller, South Dakota. Unless you're from there, you've probably never heard of it. It's really small. I couldn't wait to get out of there.

As a child, whenever someone asked me what I wanted to be when I grew up, I never told them a specific profession. My answer was always the same. "I want to be rich".

I don't know why that was my focus. I certainly didn't grow up rich. But I remember when I was young, asking my mom why an aunt was always so crabby, and she said, "Because she has to work a lot to be able to pay her bills." Somehow, at age five, that got instilled in my subconscious. I thought, "I don't want to do that." I just knew I wanted to be in control instead of letting life happen to me.

Case in point, when I was 15. I wanted to buy a car. But the only job I could get was making pizzas in the deli at the gas station. For minimum wage, which at the time was $5.15 an hour. Toward the end of my eight-hour shift, I did the math in my head and thought, "I'm not letting them put that value on my time." I was mad that someone could do that, but angrier at myself that I allowed it. So I quit. My first day was my last day.

I knew I needed a change. So I began spending summers with my sister in Minnesota, where something happened that changed my life.

My family was big in Herbalife. At 15, I got my first taste of network marketing, and I totally drank the Kool-Aid. I was transformed. By age 16, I was making a good buck. More important, I was learning and growing as a person. I knew I was going to be an entrepreneur, not an employee. I knew I had to surround myself with the right people and read the right books and learn the right things.

The day I graduated high school my bags were already packed. I walked out of my commencement, got in my car, and left South Dakota for good. I came back to Minnesota, where I've been ever since…more or less. (That's the journey part)

At 17, I decided to be a chiropractor. I could help people and make a good living. First, I went to a two-year school, got an Associate's degree in exercise science, and began doing personal fitness training, all while still working my Herbalife business.

Then one day, I came up with an idea for a sales campaign for a product line called *Shape Works*. It was one little phrase: "We pay you to lose weight." I wrote a sales script, and when people called an 800 number they heard how we paid people per pound and inch they lost. But of course they had to get on our meal plan. The call got them in the door for a consultation, and the consultation got them into a weight loss program, which I set up. Next thing you knew I was selling between $10,000 and $15,000 worth of nutritional supplements a month.

So much for being a chiropractor. No more school for me. I was barely 21 years old, making tons of money. But the problem was, this wasn't duplicable. Which is how you make it big in the network marketing industry; having a system that others can follow.

But before I could figure that out, my life took a sharp turn. Herbalife was beginning operations in Malaysia. What better way to try to duplicate a system than being on the ground level of multi-level marketing in a new country? So I booked a one-way ticket.

But I never got to Malaysia. During a 13-hour layover in Singapore, I panicked. How could I fly halfway around the world and try to set up a company's operations in a country where I didn't know anyone and didn't even know the language? I turned around and came home as a failure. Which, by the way, wouldn't be the last time.

So now what? A new career path. I got my Series 63 license and began selling life and health insurance. I was good at it. I was salesman of the month. But I hated it. I thought, "Am I really going to be an insurance salesman the rest of my life?"

Then I saw an ad that said, "In-home sales, $80,000-plus a year". It was for a home remodeling company. They told me something that has stuck with me to this day. They said 85 percent of the job was negative, because you're dealing with telemarketing leads and cold calls. You're going to go to 100 homes, and only get into 15 of them. Then you're going to make your presentation, and you might close five or six of those. But I took the job, because of that 15 percent. I knew if I focused on the positive, I'd be fine. The numbers will work out.

Once again, I was successful. For the next few years, I was their number-one or number-two rep. Once again, I was making six figures. But as I was walking into houses carrying a window, I kept thinking, "Am I really going to be a window salesman the rest of my life?"

I decided I wanted to get back into the fitness business. I didn't want to work for anyone else, so I bought a franchise. And soon realized I was working harder and making less money than any other time in my life, except for that one day making pizzas for minimum wage. I was there 16 hours a day, and at the end of the year I had nothing to show for it.

Which led to my next adventure. A friend's company was opening up operations in Mexico, and looking for a few key people to build it. I know what you're thinking. "Remember Malaysia?" But I hated what I was doing and needed a change. So I hired a manager to run my club, leased out my condo, and flew to Puerto Vallarta. For five months I worked to build that company in Mexico. It would have been great. But one day the Mexican government shut us down. We never did get the official reason.

So once again I came back to the U.S. with my tail between my legs. Since I had rented my condo I had no place to live, so now I'm sleeping on my sister's couch. I'm broke. I couldn't even sell my gym because it wasn't making any money.

"There's no failure, only feedback."

That quote helped me get through that difficult time. Because everyone fails at some point. But how you look at your failure is the most important thing. How you respond will determine your future. You can focus on the negatives and live in the victim mindset of "Poor me, " or you can understand that we control our own destiny. I realized, I couldn't let the things that are out of my control dictate the path I would take.

I've been teaching this mindset to my seven-year-old daughter. It's easy for her to get frustrated when she struggles with something new. I'm trying to teach her that we can choose to be frustrated, or we can choose to look toward something else, and try to find the positive in these situations.

So while I was crashing at my sister's, another ad caught my eye. All it said was "Work three days a week and make $10,000." I thought, "Yeah, right." But I called, met with the guy, and it led to my ultimate life-changing moment.

He did events that were sales presentations to groups of people. I was intrigued because I had always sold on a one-to-one basis. So I went to one of his events and saw him give his presentation, then pass out appointment cards to the group. The next day, he went out and met with them individually, and sold a bunch of product. I said, "Wait a minute. I only have to do one or two presentations like this a week, and sell like this? I can leverage my time?" It was the proverbial lightbulb moment.

So now the question was, "What can I sell?" I took a couple of his products, added a few additional ones, and started my first company. We went from zero to $2 million in sales, in just six months. I had to hire sales reps. In the next year we did $12 million in sales, and we did the same number again the following year.

Now I wasn't selling any more. I was booking the places and filling the rooms. My reps were doing the presentations, getting appointments, closing the deals, and turning the money in to me. It was a well-oiled machine. And it was a cash cow.

So I started looking to see what else I could sell. We added walk-in bathtubs, and did about $2 million in sales on those in the first year, with just one person selling them.

And then it hit me. I had a system. One that works really well. Remember back in my Herbalife days, when I learned a system needed to be duplicable? Now I had one. I realized I shouldn't be looking for products to sell. I should be looking for people who are passionate about what they sell but need help selling it. People who need help getting it out to the public, or want to take it to the next level.

Which is how the *Social Dynamic Selling System*™ was born. It didn't happen overnight. It took time to fine tune it, to actually create the processes that others would follow, and take everything I had learned and turn it into a course that would teach them all of that.

And here it is.

It's not just dinner

No matter what you're selling, it's a struggle to get your share of the market. Everybody is dying for a piece of the pie. The good news is no matter what your market, it's a really big pie. There will always be more people who want and need your services than you can handle.

Your challenge is finding them.

Tactics such as cold calling, door-to-door canvassing, direct mail, and traditional media work reasonably well, but the results are slow and percentages are low.

What about SEO? Only one company can be at the top of the Google rankings at any given time. So if your website is nowhere to be found on the first page, good luck. More important, Google rankings do nothing to establish you as a trustworthy or even competent business.

That's where the *Social Dynamic Selling System*™ comes in. We have taken a proven lead generation tool, re-engineered it and perfected it to work immediately, and for years to come.

The tool is dinner seminar marketing.

The industries that use it know the results are quick, they come with a spectacular ROI, and the process immediately establishes you as a trusted, go-to expert in your field. If your industry is not using it, this is your chance to stand out and gain an amazing advantage.

All those other tactics are forms of interruption marketing. They convey your message, whether or not the recipient wants to hear it. Even worse, the message is about you—soliciting their business. That's why these forms of marketing have such low response rates.

Dinner seminar marketing is different for one crucial reason—value.

The concept is simple. You invite people to a great restaurant for a free dinner, which you pay for. While they are there, you teach them something valuable about your industry. Then you ask them for the opportunity to bid on their next project.

The value you're offering is a great, free dinner and education. All they have to do is listen to what you have to say about a topic you know well. You're not selling anything at your dinner. You're building relationships. Quickly and easily.

Many of your dinner attendees will invite you into their homes for a one-on-one consultation, and you will wind up with more than enough new business to make your dinner seminar well worth the costs involved.

You'll schedule an appointment with your new leads within three days of the dinner, evaluate their need, and close the sale. Depending on your product or service, they could be a customer for life. You will become their go-to expert.

With few exceptions, everybody at your dinner is already a high quality, pre-qualified lead. The SDSS pays for itself—many times over—from the very first time you use it.

Anybody can buy leads. But you never really know what you're going to get. What you really need is a way to cultivate and collect your own leads. We teach a system that you can use to go out and find your own, much higher quality leads, literally for as long as you're in business.

The most powerful aspect of dinner seminar marketing is the credibility you create by meeting prospects face to face and demonstrating your expertise and trustworthiness in your field. You do everything you say you're going to do. The prospect comes and eats for free. You give them good information. You don't try to sell them anything. You build good will, credibility, and start building a business relationship.

When they invite you to their house for an estimate, the hard part is already over. They know you, believe what you say, and–if you've managed the process carefully and properly–like and trust you.

Dinner seminar marketing has been effectively used in many different industries for years. Financial services companies are probably the biggest fans. When you consider the lifetime value of a financial planning or insurance client against the cost of a dinner— and not even a lavish dinner at that—it quickly becomes pretty clear why dinner seminar marketing makes sense.

Financial planners and insurance pros know the value of personal relationships very, very well. That's how they grow their businesses. In their industry, there is no better way than a dinner seminar to get good leads and lucrative clients.

But these same principles apply to many other industries. What we've done is adapt this highly successful marketing tactic so anyone can easily use it. We've turned dinner seminar marketing into a science. We have perfected every aspect of it based on years of trial and error.

Your power comes from owning the event. You don't have to vie with competitors to attract attention.

Like any other effective marketing tactic, making dinner seminars work for you requires a bit of planning and organization. In the SDSS, we have organized everything you need into an easy-to-follow program that walks you through the entire process of launching a dinner-seminar marketing campaign step-by-step.

In addition to detailed explanations about each of the steps, we include:

Spreadsheets

Cost Calculators

Scripts

Templates

Worksheets

Checklists

Presentations

All these tools are integrated into a detailed, step-by-step action plan for you to use as is or customize to your own specifications. Everything is there for you and everything is ready to go.

If you follow our systematic approach to holding dinner seminars, you can start hosting your first dinner seminar campaign in less than a month -- 27 days to be exact. Many of our clients have found this so profitable, they're doing a seminar every week.

Obviously I couldn't give away the farm in this chapter. I will tell you, the SDSS leaves nothing to chance and nothing to the imagination. We tell you what to do, how to do it, when to do it, who to talk to, and what to say. Anyone can run a successful dinner seminar campaign if they follow our clear and simple approach to the letter.

The *Social Dynamic Selling* Online Academy provides all the tools you need, a detailed, step-by-step action plan for you to use as is or customize to your own specifications. Everything you need, from the moment you plan your seminar to the time you close your sales. Everything is there for you and everything is ready to go. It's plug and play.

Plus you get me. Every module is taught by me, and I will share every single step I've used to generate over $80 million of income over the past eight years.

Because you've bought this book, you're eligible for a special offer. The *Social Dynamic Selling* Online Academy retails for $3,997. And everyone who has paid that price will tell you it's worth every penny. They've gotten their investment back ten-fold, 100-fold, even more.

But you can get the entire course for just $997. All the templates, all the research, all the guidance. Years of increased profits for less than one month's mortgage payment for the average person. Just go to www.socialdynamicselling.com/book to sign up.

And here's one other added bonus for you. When you buy the course for the special reduced price, you also get a 30-minute Strategy Session call with me. A half hour of one-on-one time. We'll go over your goals and how to reach them. Your challenges and how to overcome them. Business owners pay $10,000 for a one-day session with me. You'll get this 30-minute session at no cost.

I'm on a mission to help business owners, entrepreneurs, sales people and others create a predictable, sustainable, and scalable source of revenue for their business. The *Social Dynamic Selling System*™ is my way of doing that.

***

To Contact Rylee

Rylee Meek PNLP, PTT, CCHt, CSC

Practitioner of NLP, Practitioner of TIME Techniques, Certified Clinical Hypnotherapist, Certified Success Coach

http://workwithrylee.com/

http://socialdynamicselling.com/

https://go.socialdynamicselling.com/enroll-now

https://www.instagram.com/ryleemeek7/

https://www.linkedin.com/in/rylee-meek-1556a919/

https://www.facebook.com/TheRyleeMeek/

https://twitter.com/ryleemeek

Charol Messenger

Charol Messenger is a visionary author, with thirteen book awards, including two international first place, *You 2.0* (2016) and *The New Humans* (2017). *Intuition for Every Day* includes dozens of personal stories as well as original techniques for how to access what is inborn in everyone. *Wings of Light* includes how to find a lost loved one. Charol's many inspiring books began coming to her following her auspicious shift into heightened awareness in 1975. Charol is also a professional writer and editor. She has published 220 articles, book reviews, essays, and poetry in Canada, L.A., Denver and Colorado Springs newspapers, writers' journals, social clubs, and college journals. Her international newsletter *Global Citizen* 1987-88 earned her recognition from Colorado Governor Roy Romer and author Richard Bach.

Her professional writing began in 1969 as an advertising assistant, writing copy. With a B.A. from the University of Colorado in 1985, she began full-time freelance book editing in 1994. Her 1,458 professional projects include writing 147 corporate projects (13 manuals). Freelance includes 244 books (65 memoirs, 45 nonfiction, 90 novels): 2 fully ghostwritten (expanded), 14 fully developed/rewritten, 153 substantive line-edited, and 37 Ph.D. dissertations copyedited.

How to Live Stress Free

By Charol Messenger, International Award-Winning Visionary
Author

It used to take me a long time to figure things out. I worried about everything, and I made a lot of mistakes. I still do at times. However, once I get it, it stays with me forever. Here are a few personal stories of how I learned not to let things get to me and to trust and act upon the insights that come *to* me for guidance—as they do for all of us, in all of life's decisions and concerns.

Aside from a spontaneous awakening November 1975 to my higher destiny and purpose, one of the first times the inner *magic* guided me (and I listened) was when it *came* to me in 1979 that I really needed to quit that job. I was sure. On Friday, I gave notice, after three-and-a-half years as the senior word-processor at ITU in Colorado Springs. Then immediately I wondered, what could I do now for money? Inner voice answered, *Do readings.* OMG. *That's a good idea,* I thought back, as I already had been giving free soul readings for a while now. Then the next Monday—I got a phone call from a lawyer, who had been tracking me down for five years, with a $5,000 inheritance from my deceased mother (who had been murdered in front of me when I was two, but I never knew her family). Well – I was already clear on just what to do with the money: It was meant to support me while I started my new path of giving soul readings.

That's when I learned to trust my gut. And doing so has been the right decision (after the fact) every single time I have faced a choice. I get a very strong feeling that I need to do this or that (or a very clear certainty to say no). The feeling overwhelms me. It fills me. And I feel linked to something auspicious in that moment—though I have no idea where it will take me, or how I will pay the bills, or even WHY I'm doing it. I just know I HAVE TO. So I say YES! I jump. I take that next step without doubt, without question. It is *after*

I accept and act that I find out *why* I did this (always good) and what happens next (always a surprise and amazing).

So, basically, in seventy-three years, I have found that the real secret to life (or at least peace of mind, no worry, not to sweat the small stuff and often not even the big stuff) is to trust your gut. Because we DO know when it is the right step, the right choice. We all do. We are born with this instinct.

My next big discovery was when I quit my job in the spring of 1994. It was a long-term temp job with CDOT in Denver Metro. After six months (though they were good to me, and they let me edit and write and organize anything I wanted for them), I felt like a fish out of water in a desk job. I just *knew* I had to leave and focus on my deeper Self. I yearned to reconnect with the deep inner stillness. So I gave notice. Then I wondered, what would I do now for money? And inner voice answered, *Unemployment.* Ah, that's a good idea, I thought back. So I had enough money coming in over the next six months that I never once gave a thought to money (the one and only time in my life) and I focused *all* of my attention on daily deep two-hour meditations, seeking to reconnect with my inner Self.

Then something unexpected happened. After seven weeks, new insights suddenly started pouring out of me: five books in five months. It was incredible! And all on how we are born with gifts and can remember who we really are. These books were the real beginning of my new path as a visionary author, and I had not seen it coming. I had only felt my heart urging me to reconnect. Never before had I done two-hour meditations, certainly not every day. This all was very unusual. This unexpected connection to my soul consciousness was a whole new level of awareness. I now know it came from trusting myself, my deep need to connect to my inner self, and acting in faith.

Just as I finished the last of the five books in September 1994, the unemployment money ran out and that was the first time I once again gave money a thought. What was I going to do now? And inner voice responded, *Freelance edit.* So the next day, I placed a classified ad in *The Denver Post*—and immediately I had money coming in. That was the beginning of my freelance editing, which I've been doing ever since (as my day job).

So, I was beginning to learn who I was and am, learning to trust my instincts, which always had led me into better situations than I had imagined and into many amazing experiences.

For example, my tan border collie Che: When I was still living in Colorado Springs. I had gotten her at three months old from a young couple. However, after a year, apartment living was not for her. So I placed a newspaper ad in the *Colorado Springs Gazette.* The first people I gave her to told me they lived in the country. However, I soon learned they had lied about the country-home environment, so I went and took her back. Her happiness and well-being were my responsibility. But I was still in the apartment, so I tried again to find a home for Che. This time, a woman said that she and her two children and husband lived up in the mountains in Woodland Park. I was delighted that Che would have a good life.

Just after they took her home—I left on a six-week Amtrak adventure, round trip through Las Vegas, up the coast of California (doing occasional readings in places where I knew people), to Lake Tahoe, then back to Colorado. Here's where the instincts came in: The *entire* time I was gone, I was having nightmares about Che being abandoned and feeling her terror. So as soon as I returned, a coworker Jan and I drove up to Woodland Park to look for Che. I had the address but the house was empty and boarded up. I got the landlord's phone number off the door and called, and he asked me to come visit. He had Che. It turned out that right after the family had taken Che home, they had moved to California—and left the dog locked up inside the house without food or water, and had told no one. It was weeks before the landlord discovered Che.

But now Che was with a good home, kids, horses, other dogs—and happy. I told them that if they ever decided not to keep her, to call me and I would come get her. Two years later, I had just moved to a rental house when they did call. I immediately got into my car, drove up and brought Che home. We had a deep connection. Her spirit had reached out to me when she was in trouble, and I had gotten the message. After that, whenever I took a trip and left her at home with a sitter, in my dreams I checked on Che to make sure she was alright—and she was, every time. After the check-in, no more dreams about her and no worries. I *knew* she was okay.

I share this experience because it's about trusting the connection that we all have—every one of us—especially with those we love. We are all connected.

Here's another dog story: My shy, floppy-eared miniature schnauzer Cabra got lost, first as a puppy (four more times over the years, even at age fourteen). The first time it happened, my friend Jan and I had met at a park and I wasn't paying attention to Cabra— who was not on a leash (bad mommy). Suddenly, I realized she wasn't there. Jan and I looked all over the park for an hour and couldn't find her. After Jan left for work, it was *then* that the first really magical experience happened: It suddenly *came* into my awareness *exactly* what to do, say, and visualize. So I did. Right there, on the park bench. I focused on this new ritual and continued it for over an hour, in deep focus— until suddenly a peace flowed *into* me and I *knew* all was okay and that, whatever happened, Cabra would be okay. I let go and went home.

As soon as I entered my rental condo, the phone was ringing. Someone had picked up Cabra (ID tag). Even though she had crossed downtown rush-hour traffic, she was safe and unharmed. I immediately rushed to get her, feeling that angels had indeed protected her *and* had sent me the insights on exactly how to bring her home safely. And this worked *every* other time for my wandering silver-haired sweetie, whom I didn't know was deaf.

Trusting the Universe is something I have learned is essential to life. With each extraordinary experience (many more than I can share here), I have been given what to do and say, and *every* time has had a miraculous result. For example, when I was still in Colorado Springs, at my two-level condo at the foot of Cheyenne Mountain (where Norad is) . . .

One night, I was ironing and watching TV when there was a *News Alert! Flash Flood. Evacuate Now!* First, I scrambled around crazily, trying to think what to pack, fast. In my big office, I looked at all the manuscripts not yet typed, a life's work. Then with a sudden *certainty,* I just stopped. There was no way I was going to leave these manuscripts behind! And what about my two dogs? Then a force of *knowing* just came over me, more powerful than ever before. With clarity, I walked room to room and thrust my arms out with force and intention, declaring, *"This will not be!"* I visualized protection around my condo and my car—until peace flowed into me and I *knew* all would be well. I stopped then, turned on the TV and forgot all about the storm.

The next morning, my half of the duplex condo was the only home for several blocks all around that was NOT flooded. My condo neighbor's basement was, mine was not. One caveat: In the Intention and visualization, I had forgotten to include the little fenced side yard—AND the dog house had been moved several feet and the fence torn out, but my house and car were dry, and my dogs and I were safe and unharmed.

I share these stories because I know now, at my core, that *every* person has incredible powers accessible to us. We have only to listen—to the strong feelings that come over us and to the counsel within.

Another incredible event was the tornado that skipped *my* house *only*. I was working in downtown Denver in a high-rise office building as a long-term clerical temp about 1990. On the radio in my cubicle, suddenly, *News Alert! Tornado!* Passing right through my neighborhood in Northglenn, down my street—an hour north by bus! Oh, my! My dogs were there, and Che was outside. What was I going to do?! Then suddenly a powerful premonition came over me and, with it, the same *knowing* of just what to do, say, and visualize. So, I did. Right there, behind my cubicle walls, whispering with force—and I continued until it felt *done* and the peace flowed *into* me and I *knew* all was well. And it was.

At the end of the work day, when I got home—it was obvious. The tornado had taken out the fence on the west side of my backyard—had gone *up* over my yard—then taken out the east fence. Che was bedraggled, wet, and terrified when she crawled out from the dog house—but she was okay! Then the TV news confirmed. Yes, indeed, the tornado had gone right down my street. Wow.

Bottom line. This is all about listening to ourselves, our world, and those around us. *And* taking *action* when our *core* instincts urge us to do so. And it is *always* right.

This is not unique to me. I listened. I accepted. I acted. Without hesitation. If I hadn't, everything would have turned out differently.

It is the many experiences like these that have taught me, again and again, to trust, to trust whatever is guiding me (that guides us all). When I do, that is how I am able to let go without worry. That doesn't mean do things that will get me into trouble; that means don't do those things, trust my instincts.

We don't have to worry about the little things. And we can train ourselves not to worry about the big things (like survival and income). When we are able to let go—and still be creative, still seek solutions—solutions arrive. Always. We have only to believe—and act upon what we *do* know and what we *can* do. The rest follows when we are ready for the next step.

When we trust our strong emotional inner pushes (soul talking to us) and we feel an inexplicable conviction, a certainty, and we vocalize it (don't keep it to yourself); and when we are in alignment with our heart calling, consistently and persistently day in and day out—that is when Miracles come to us. They just show up. When we are ready. This Energy has guided me every step of my life, even when I didn't know it.

We are all born with an innate knowing of when something is right to do (and when it isn't). We have only to trust that inner truth—and act on it. When we do, the reason for that action becomes clear to us, afterwards. *Then* leads to something better. Every step is forward.

This is how we can let go of trying to make things happen. When we are just doing our work—our passion, our talents—to our fullest possible best, day in and day out—*that* is when we are open to magical moments, opportunities, coming *to* us. They just show up. When we are listening, feeling, and are present—in that moment we know: *This is for me. This is it. This I must do. This I am doing.* When we are practiced in listening to our instinct, our inner voice—

we are able to let go of worry. We just live now, today, doing the thing we are in life to do.

In that is our magic. In that is our peace of mind. In that we find our inner calm and our joy—and our zest for the thing we were born to do. This is how we discover our innate power, to know when to say YES and when to say NO. When we are living from our heart, with the intention to do good, to help others (using our talents), this is when we are free. Free to be just who we are. And that is inner peace—Also, excitement. Because it is thrilling, every time, when the magic happens.

It feels like magic. It feels miraculous. Actually, it is the natural *consequence* of—every day—living our commitment to being who we were born to be. We are all born to be unique, yet loving. Original, yet caring. We are all born to share the light that is in us. As we light the world with our talents, thinking of others more than ourselves, we are also lighting the way of the path before us—which opens and unfolds with every step we take.

Life is a journey lived in the moments when we are present and using the gifts born in and through us. They are our legacy. We are here to give. And in that we are able to live each day with peace in our hearts and compassion for all around us. We are here as blessings in the world. Our bounty is the light we shine simply by being who we are. And in that we are everything we came into life to be.

This is our task: to trust who we already are, and be it.

My first gift from the Universe was my Tahoe friend getting my house loan for me in downtown Denver. The second was getting myself a reverse mortgage (a year ago). The third was a happenstance email for an editing job—that instead turned out to be the invitation from Jim Britt to be a co-author in his new book. And once I had read his bio on Amazon and all that he has done—I *knew,* without question, *YES. This is it.*

As Jim said to me during the call, as we chatted, "We are all connected. We are all the same energy. We are all one." This philosophy is totally in sync with what I have learned, from within. I didn't need those words to convince me, but they were another indicator that, *This is the one. And I'm ready. I am finally ready.* And I am. I have done my work, day in and day out, year after year. And now it is here, all that I have expected to *come* to me, and it has. Again. And each time it feels like the heavens have opened up and the angels sang, shining their light all over the world. And *this* is a life blessed. With a peaceful mind and open heart, all things are possible.

***

https://www.charolmessenger.com

Charol@charolmessenger.com

www.amazon.com/Charol-Messenger/e/B00A9I0ZPI

www.facebook.com/Charolm99

www.podcastmessengerofthedivine.com

Jeffrey Flack

Developing transformational healthcare leadership

Jeffrey Flack, Inc CEO and founder Certified John Maxwell Speaker, Teacher, Executive coaching, 2016. Master's in science and management and organizational behavior, Benedictine 2014. BA Management and Leadership, Judson University, 1999. Developing transformational healthcare leadership.

Dynamic Executive with over 20 years' experience managing staff and patients to desired outcomes. Visionary leader capable of defining solutions to complex patient care issues. Drives revenue growth by marketing clinical services to both physicians and clients. A transformational change agent who helps organizations transform by improving processes and interpersonal interactions. Trusted advisor on numerous health care institution leadership boards; effective group facilitator and leadership coach. Experienced in lean, Myers Briggs facilitator and worked with DISC.

A noted speaker and consultant about these and other topics of interest:
Colleague engagement let's get the players on the team.
Management worked great in the industrial revolution, now it's leadership.
Communication let's talk about this.
Diversity, we just need to change some things to work better.
Purpose, is it the needle in the haystack?
Executive Certified John Maxwell Speaker, Teacher, Executive coaching, 2016
Master's in science and management and organizational behavior, Benedictine 2014
BA Management and Leadership, Judson University, 1999

Leadership

By Jeffrey Flack

The first question that is commonly asked is, are leaders born or are they made? Now the obvious sarcastic response is, of course they all are born—I've never known a leader to be hatched or grown in a petri dish—but leaders are made. There are certain qualities and traits that are in common among leaders such as confidence and charisma, and research has even shown height to be a genetic advantage as well, but all those things won't make you a leader; there is much more to it than that. I grew up in a family of entrepreneurs who were strong leaders in their fields. This environment not only conditioned me to strive to be a leader but gave me an innate drive that seemed to be in my DNA. I didn't start out as a leader but, instead, was pulled toward it. Through my career in Physical Therapy I was driven to join committees and meet with CEO's, thus sparking a fascination with leadership and making my work environment(s) the best that it could be. Through those efforts, I've learned from many CEO's and great leaders in the field and have migrated toward studying leadership and making it my career to teach those who are willing to learn. In healthcare, many times it's the best therapist or nurse who gets promoted to management. This does not necessarily make them a great leader and can lead to frustration, not only for them, but for those who are being led. It is immediately apparent, when entering an organization, by the mentality of the staff, the service received, and the attention toward quality, what type of leader it has. Leaders are made, and I'll tell you how.

Leaders are authentic. To be authentic is to do the right thing all the time and to do what you say. Great leaders start somewhere and usually not the top. That means doing a great job wherever you are in your career and doing it consistently. If you want to be a great leader you must be a great beginner. That means showing up to work on time and working. That means not lingering in the coffee lounge for 10 minutes, chatting with staff then checking your personal emails and maybe taking a bathroom break before starting in on work. That is not the path to becoming an authentic leader. That will keep you frustrated and questioning why others are receiving promotions and you are not. Great leaders are authentic, and those are the ones people go to when they want an honest answer. They will give you a straight answer and you know the source is authentic. Being authentic is being the same person inside the organization and out. Just as you wouldn't want to see your married minister at a strip club, you would also not want to see your investment broker spends his afternoons at the casino.

Being authentic is doing and saying what is truthful and abiding by those standards in all areas of life. Many leaders have fallen by losing sight of this rule and often, never recover once it is broken. Being authentic is telling your staff the truth and modeling that as a character trait. If you aren't authentic you will not lead.

Leaders are humble. I learned that quickly. The title doesn't make the man or woman; the man or woman makes the title. I'm sure everyone has worked for someone incompetent and were managed by title, not by leadership. Those are the people who introduce themselves by title first and then by name. These people have little to no respect from their staff and are usually are the butt of the joke as soon as they leave the room. There is a story of a cruise ship captain who was in a deep fog and saw lights in front of him. On his intercom, he called out to the lights ahead, "This is Captain Ego, and you need to steer left as we are headed your way." The response was, "*You* need to steer left." The great captain, now enraged, yelled through the intercom, "This is Captain Ego, captain of the largest cruise ship ever built, housing thousands of guests, and I command you to steer left!" The response was, "This is Tom, sole keeper of this lighthouse, and you are advised to steer left before you sink your ship." Being humble is a virtue which allows you to get close to your people as a leader and avoid trouble. There were many occasions when I met CEO's on the hospital floor, and they introduced themselves by name only because I was new and we hadn't met me before. They simply wanted to know who I was and what I did and welcomed me to the team. Afterward, when I questioned a hospital worker who that was, I was informed, "That's the CEO; he's always like that. He just wants to know everyone, and he's a good guy."

Being humble is being a leader. Managing by title is not leading and can be seen as autocratic.

Leaders are stewards. Jack Welch, CEO of GE, once stated in a seminar that once you become a leader you are now working for the people and no longer for yourself. He also said you must be strong enough to lead others who don't want to be on your team to pursue other opportunities on someone else's team. His management style throughout his career at GE was to typically cut the bottom 10% of low performers. Jim Collins stated in his book, *Good to Great,* "you need get the right people on your bus and let the wrong ones off at the next stop You work for the people, but they have to be the right people. That means listening to your people. When I was directing staff, the first thing–the first thing I would do was to meet each member one-on-one. I had them answer a 5-question questionnaire so that I get to know them and find out their needs.

Why did you choose to work for this organization?

What do you love about your position and our team?

Where would you like to go in your career in the next 5 years?

What changes would make this a better place to work?

How can I help you with reaching these goals?

These questions helped me to understand each individual better. I could tell if they liked what they did and were proud of their organization. I could tell if they were problem-solvers. I understood if they were comfortable in what they did and had the tools to be successful. I knew if they wanted to stay where they were or grow into something else. This also allowed me to get a feel of the organization and what challenges needed to be addressed. Great leaders know they are working for their team. It's the team that produces all the results. It's the team that interacts with customers, and it's the team that interacts with the community. Once you understand that you are building a team, you are leaning into leadership.

Aristotle said, "The soul never thinks without a picture." Passionate leaders have a vision. Great leaders know that something needs to change, and they have a vision as to how it should be and a plan ~~on~~ as to how to get there. Great leaders never work a day in their life; they are so passionate about what they do, it's not work. Great leaders don't dread waking up, driving to work, or the work week ahead. They do what they do because they love what they do, and they do it to make things just a little bit better for everyone. If you don't love what you are doing, why are you doing it? Because it pays the bills, because it's the only thing you know, because you're too old to change now? I worked full-time in Physical Therapy while simultaneously studying and receiving a bachelor's degree in Management and Leadership, while married with two children. Then, working full-time, I went back to school and received a master's degree in Management and Organizational Behavior. It was tough, but I had a vision to learn more about business and leadership so that I could attain my goal of becoming a better leader. I did it because I loved learning about leadership? It was work but didn't feel like it. I am passionate about leadership and teaching others. It's something I think about all the time and how I can continually get better at it.

Leaders are great at what they do. That means they have the abilities and the knowledge and practice getting better at what they do best. Prince, the pop star, was a lover of basketball and wanted to be a basketball player but at 5 foot 2 and 120 lbs., that probably wouldn't have worked out, so he immersed himself in music. He played for hours and hours, day after day, learning new instruments along the way and became, arguably, one of the best musicians there ever was. He was great at what he did. My best leaders were great at what they did and practiced getting better at their craft all the time. They were constantly learning to hone the saw. According to Malcom Gladwell, author of the book, *Outliers*, it takes 10,000 hours of deliberate practice to become great at something. ~~However~~, it has been recently suggested in the book, *The Click Moment*, that one would only have a 1% chance of improving after 10,000 hours of practice. I argue that if you take a leader who has invested 10,000 hours of practice into improving his or her game versus a new leader, the experienced leader will have more than a 1% chance of performing better. Also, if an entrepreneur has spent 10,000 hours in their business, they will have learned the rules of the road or will have gone out of business. Great leaders are great at what they do and continue to improve and adapt or go extinct. Take for example some of the great chain stores versus the behemoth Amazon. The leaders of chains such as Sears, K-mart, Toys-R-Us weren't so great at what they did. Perhaps they were great in their time, but they went extinct. Great leaders are great at what they do and continue to grow to stay on top.

Leaders have emotional intelligence. I've worked in the healthcare industry for 27 years, and if I didn't improve my emotional intelligence I would not? be in therapy for sure. When one works amongst people who are sick, hurt, and dying, they are not usually at their best. I've worked with a wide variety of patients in physical therapy, trauma orthopedic joint replacement, general surgical, and mental health, and in all types of rehab settings. They might not have the best manners or comments when you work with them. Yet, I motivated people to do things they didn't want to do as a result of emotional intelligence. I've been bitten, had my hair pulled, been grabbed where I didn't want to be grabbed, kicked, spit on, peed on, and yes, defecated on. I've also been sworn at, threatened, and told to stick objects up unmentionable places. Dealing with that take's emotional intelligence. In fact, I learned it so well was so skilled at it that I began to get all of the challenging patients. Later, I was promoted to a position in which I taught staff the communication skills necessary to deal with peers, families, irate physicians, and patients. I became a leader in and a mentor to many groups in emotional intelligence. Steven Covey, best known for his book, the *7 Habits of Highly Effective People*, states that one must "seek to understand before being understood." A main problem in healthcare is that staff rush in to do the task and don't treat the patient as a human. It's not intentional, it's just that they think they are saving lives and the task is more important than person. John Maxwell has stated, "It's not how much you know, it's how much care before anyone will want to work for you or trust you." If you don't love people and don't develop your emotional intelligence, then you shouldn't go into leadership because you must care and listen to be a great leader.

Leaders are constant learners. I've touched on this throughout the chapter because it is so important. It's been stated that a bachelor's degree has about a 5-year longevity and then is outdated. It's even less than that in certain fields because technology changes so rapidly. Forty-two percent of high school graduates never read a book after graduating. Thirty-three percent of college graduates never read a book after graduating. Now this is a bit sad for the education of our society but gives those an advantage who do read. I read a book a week and it's on learning about something new in business, leadership, and/or self-improvement. All the great leaders I worked for had books they were reading and buying for the management staff. The best ones would teach on the subject. Many of them would have workshops with committees and would interact to learn the subject matter. I like to look at what Bill Gates is reading as he has his top 5 listed annually. I've read most of ~~his~~ John Maxwell's books, but he keeps writing them, so I'm a bit behind. Dave Ramsey has recommendations and his peers, who are leaders, are always sharing their favorites. I also make notes and put tabs in books so that I can quickly reference good ideas or techniques that I've come across. TED Talks are great to watch versus playing candy crush on your phone. They are 18-minute-long seminars on topics you can choose from leaders in their field. YouTube is also a sanctuary for learning; you can type in *leadership* and thousands of speakers are available at a click: Jack Welch, Bill Gates, John Maxwell, Les Brown, Tony Robbins; the list goes on and on.

Great leaders are great learners. Great leaders have coaches and mentors and go to continuing education as well. I'm in John Maxwell's mentorship program right now and can listen daily ~~on~~ as to how to build my business, market it, and refine it. I'm with a network of people who I can reach out to and troubleshoot with if something isn't working well. The more you invest in yourself, the better the return. Leadership is about learning and teaching and learning and teaching. Business models change, generations change, and the world changes, so if you aren't changing, you're retiring.

My Grandfather was a stout, god-fearing man who worked from sun up until sun down. He had one speed, which was redline fast, and started and stopped at that same speed daily. His farm spanned 100 acres and had two large ponds on it that he utilized for Sunday fishing after church. This was his relaxing time and the time that I would spend asking the childhood question, "Grandpa, why do you work so hard? This seems like more fun." His answer was direct, without hesitation, and driven from a teachable standpoint. "The ground isn't going to plant itself, the cows are not going to milk themselves, and the weeds are not going to pick themselves. The corn, the beans, are not going to harvest themselves, and the grain is not going to drive itself to the silos, Jeff. I work hard because there is no other way to get what you want out of life. I could fish and let a day go by, and the ground will wait but the season of growing won't. I could let the cows dry up and then I wouldn't have to milk them but then we wouldn't have milk, butter, nor cheese. I could let the weeds grow and choke out the crops but then we wouldn't have a plentiful harvest to buy seed for the next season for planting. All these things I could let go but then they would disappear just as the fish would if we fished them daily. For everything there is a season and that requires hard work, Jeff. That is the reason I work so hard."

My grandpa and grandma on my father's side bought a dry-cleaning business which they owned successfully for decades, in which my grandma wouldn't retire from altering until she was 92. I asked them one day at the cleaners why they thought they were so successful in town. My grandpa stated, "Because we do good work," and was laughing. My grandma retorted, "We do *excellent* work every time or we don't charge. In fact, if it isn't perfect, it isn't Flack quality, and we are not allowed to charge." This is not an exaggeration; my grandma and grandpa are perfectionists. In fact, their house looks like it just came out of a magazine to this day; everything is meticulously in its place. That message of quality was permanently stamped in my memory.

My father was a top salesman for many companies and had a trophy room in his office—Rookie of the Year in sales, Top Salesman multiple years over. He finally acquired his own business and shot to the stars with it. I asked him one day, home from college, "What do you think the key to success in business is, Dad? I mean, you have multiple titles of Top Salesman in every company you ever worked, and now you have your own business, and some major retail companies will only work with you. What is the secret?" His reply, "Tell the truth." "What? That's it?" I asked. "It's not some complicated sales funnel or psychological chess game? It's not discounts or volume price breaks? 'Tell the truth?' I thought everyone did that, tell the truth that is." "Nope," he said. "Most sales people will tell people what they want to hear and won't get the repeat sale. I tell truth and build trust and a following."

***

Instagram www.instagram.com/jeffreyflackceo/?hl=en

Facebook www.facebook.com/jeffreyflackI/

Twitter www.twitter@jeffreyflack3

Website www.workwithjeffreyflack.com

Email jeffrey@workwithjeffreyflack.com

Editor Lisa Motolla Hudon www.lisamattolahudon.com

Mark Recker

Mark Recker attended a year of college after high school, but was eventually drawn towards the auto industry. He applied and tested for a skilled tradesman apprenticeship, earning himself a Journeyman card in the mechanical trades in record time. He later thirsted for more knowledge and returned to college studying business administration.

Mark is also the successful inventor of an exercise apparatus that received a United States patent. His creativity as an out-of-the-box thinker did not stop there. He applied his talent towards building successful down-lines in network marketing. His passion for problem solving and helping others succeed has earned him respect as a true leader in the network marketing industry.

Currently sitting on the advisory board for a prominent health and wellness company, Mark actively works to market nutritional products that aid in adult stem cell production and weight loss.

Mark credits his success to the work ethic and responsibility he learned growing up on a 600-acre farm and his competitiveness in high school sports. He enjoys being in nature, relaxing on a beach, and spending time with his wonderful wife Marilyn. He has three grown children and four grandchildren.

If You Can Dream It, You Can Achieve It

By Mark Recker

My desire to become an entrepreneur started around the age of 15. I remember helping my father set up our tractor for fall plowing. We had to clamp an extra tire onto the existing wheel for added traction. While clamping on the tire, my father pointed out that the clamps were patented by a fellow farmer who owned a machine shop and made a lot of money from it. After hearing that, I told my father that someday I would patent something too. Fast forward 20 years later, November of 1998, and I was being awarded a patent on an exercise apparatus. If you can dream it, you can achieve it, as long as you never give up.

First came the Gold Rush, and then came the Internet. During the Gold Rush, people selling the tools and supplies made a fortune, and many miners returned home empty-handed. Today, network marketing could offer one of the quickest ways to build wealth for those who wish to mine the Internet by using teamwork, leveraging, and duplication as their tools of choice. It's important to know how to use these tools so that you can achieve network marketing success.

People are naturally drawn to the idea of being part of a group or team environment, and to being able to share in success together. It's important to work as a team, leverage, and duplicate to achieve success. After I entered into multi-level marketing, it didn't take me long to figure out something was broken and needed to be fixed. I approached the CEO of the company I work for and asked for some flexibility to try a new team concept approach. I promised him that I would run everything by him for approval, so he agreed to let me do it. My first task was to develop a team website and Facebook group. I secured a website domain using the company's name, with the word "team" behind it. If I was going to emphasize my new concept of teamwork, leveraging, and duplication, then my domain name needed to reflect that. I built the following pages: Join, Blog, Members, Tag My Lead, and Show Me Proof. I soon discovered that people were attracted to this type of team concept. I also rationalized that if the failure rate in network marketing really was around 95%, as some claim it is, then capturing a percentage of that group would make any person extremely wealthy.

As a result of this approach, approximately 63% of the employees in this company now report to me, and my personal down-line retention rate remains extremely high. Zig Ziglar was right, "If you help enough people get what they want, then you will get what you want." I had finally cracked the code to network marketing success.

Stories Tell and Stories Sell

Now that I had my team website and Facebook page built, I needed to attract like-minded people and educate them about my concept of teamwork, leveraging, and duplication. It's important to brand yourself and your concept when introducing your ideas to others. Capturing the attention of your prospect is a challenge, so you have to find a unique way to do this and earn their trust. I remembered a story from my childhood my mother once read to me. This story helped shape my future. It was about a character who was lazy and did not like to work to save up money to buy food for the winter. When winter came, the character ran out of food. I remember a picture of the character holding a fork and staring at one last green pea on his plate. His kitchen cabinets were wide open and empty, and he had a look of despair on his face. There was even a mouse in the picture who was also clearly worried about its next meal. I told my mother I never wanted that to happen to me, and she told me to work hard and save so it never would. I realized stories would be my means of getting my message out. I set out to introduce my concept of teamwork, leveraging, and duplication by blogging creative stories. The very first story I wrote on my blog was called, "Dead Flock of Geese Found in Farmer's Field." Here it is with an updated title:

Ebola Virus Found in Dead Flock of Geese

A flock of geese took off for the south as winter arrived. Before setting off, they all argued with each other about the right flight plan, what time of day to leave, what altitude to fly at, and which wind current to ride on. They refused to come to an agreement on the best flight plan. As each goose took its turn in the lead, it would change in the direction that it felt was best. After three days of non-stop flying, the geese had finally reached their destination. However, something didn't look right, and they soon realized they had landed in the same field they had taken off from. Unfortunately, they were too tired and weak to make a second attempt to go south, and the snow set in. The geese ended up starving and froze to death. An autopsy report cited the real cause of death as "lack of teamwork and leveraging" because "everyone was talking and nobody was listening."

Author: Mark Recker 2018

The story was a hit, and people started to take notice because they could relate to the difficulty of network marketing. Some called me about my opportunity, and some joined me as a result. Each story I wrote included a summary to reinforce the idea that teamwork, leveraging, and duplication are the only way to make money from home in network marketing. I also linked keywords within the stories for search engine optimization. I even had my team members join me in a game of Follow the Leader, where they would visit the same social sites I did and give me a positive comment or thumbs up. This way, they could brand themselves and leave their affiliate links behind on the comment pages. This also helped our team website rank higher in search results.

Members Page

Having a member's page on your team website shows evidence of your success and builds trust. Encourage your team members to set up their personal profiles along with any affiliate links. This way, they can invite others to the team website and have them join through the member's page by clicking on their affiliate link. You want to drive traffic to one team website so you rank higher on searches. Your focus should be in helping others succeed as a team; this method reinforces your team concept. Depending on what type of tools your website offers, your membership page could serve as a great communication tool for members. Make it a habit to communicate with your team members on a weekly basis and hold webinars on your team concept.

Members can then invite prospects to the webinar to learn more about your team concept.

Blog Page

A blog page is necessary for promoting your concept for team building and increasing your website ranking in searches. This is where you get to brand yourself as a leader and help your members build their down-lines. I use this for posting creative stories to help reinforce my concept of teamwork, leveraging, and duplication. I also place these blog articles on other social sites and link key phrases and keywords back to my team website. This increases traffic, website ranking, and helps build the down-line.

Show Me The Proof Page

The Show Me The Proof page is for building trust for anyone visiting our team website.

Co-op members can visit this page to access the team rotator stats url to verify their placement and monitor traffic. New prospects that are placed in the team rotator for 30 days of free advertising can also verify their placement and monitor their traffic. New members are required to fill out the form on our home page in order to be added to our team rotator and take advantage of the 30 days of free advertising. The 30 days begin immediately once they join, so it's important that they provide their information as soon as they join. It's the responsibility of their up-line co-op sponsor to inform them about these details.

Join page

The Join Page is basically a place where a person can click on a Sign Up button that is connected to our team rotator. I added this page because some people complained they could not find the place to join within the home page content. Apparently, they did not read everything over to find the numerous active links where they could have clicked to join. The lesson learned here is, don't take things for granted and make sure you are very specific on how to sign up. Place a 'Join" page tab at the far left menu bar because people normally read left to right.

Leveraging Your Advertising Co-op

Leveraging provides you with the ability to increase your wealth in the shortest amount of time. Your goal as a leader is to help your down-line make money, so you'll make money too. After you've gone through your contact list, you'll need to develop some type of sales funnel to maintain growth. Consider forming an advertising co-op with team members who are willing to participate. Many fail in network marketing because they fail to maintain a list of prospects. They also get burned out chasing after people, trying to convince them to join their opportunity. Your main objective is to get others chasing you instead of you chasing them. So sell your idea, not the opportunity, and you will see better results.

Is it necessary to have an advertising co-op? Let me ask you this: If you were going to start a painting business, you would have to invest in paintbrushes, rollers, ladders, vehicle, tarps, and cleaning supplies. Now, how would you get the word out about your business? You would have to advertise, right? Then why should it be any different as a networker wanting to work from home? Affordability becomes the key issue here, so consider leveraging the cost of your advertising through the use of a co-op.

When advertising, make sure you test your ads for the best results. Most advertisers will tell you that consistency is important, so choose the right types of magazines for your ad. For example, if you're promoting a business opportunity, then place your ad in a small business opportunity magazine. I always like to have an ad running every month for consistency and recommend running them for a period of 3 months. Then, you can evaluate your ad and decide if you need to change it up or find another place to advertise. I also prefer magazine ads because they have a longer shelf life. People have a tendency to save a magazine, as opposed to a letter or postcard mailed to them. Magazines are easy to carry around or store without forgetting where you left it.

Determine a dollar amount for each member. If you don't receive enough revenue to cover your advertisement costs, one possibility is to offer additional co-op shares to your team members. Let's say you allow a team member to purchase up to four shares for $25 each. One person decides to purchase all four shares for $100. So for them, you would set the rotator ratio at 4:1—compared to 1:1 for the person purchasing only one $25 share. Therefore, they would receive four times the traffic as the person who only purchased one share.

Now, before I go further, let me explain what a rotator is. A rotator is a software program that rotates members' affiliate links within the team. It's not that difficult to use, and you can go on YouTube to find instructions on how to set one up. When people see that your goal as a team is to help others succeed, they are more likely to sign up.

Tag My Lead Page

Now, you have a co-op in place and you've found an advertiser to take co-op members' payments. Make it a requirement that they send in their own payments to the advertiser and have them write your co-op information on the payments for the advertiser to track. Set a date when co-op funds are due to the advertiser based on when the ads run. With the team co-op ads that I run, I use my phone number, so the contact can leave their information on my voicemail. Then, I add these leads to our password-protected 'Tag My Lead' page on our team website. Co-op members then tag the leads by filling out a form. If the lead is available, I assign it to them. If the lead they requested is taken, I assign them a different one. Set up your phone's voicemail to ask for a person's full name, mailing address, email, and phone number. I always let calls go to my voicemail so that my co-op members can call back requesting clarification on a contact's mailing information. This is the first step in the qualifying process and in creating a personal relationship built on trust. If they don't call back to verify their information, one has to wonder how serious they really are. At this point, I let my co-op members have the final say on whether they want to send the lead any additional information or cut them loose.

The Follow-Up

When a person responds to your ad, they are actually asking for help.

The two most effective phrases to say to your prospect are, "I am so sorry," and "how can I help you."

One day, while calling some leads, I experimented with using this and was amazed at how many of my leads opened up to my opportunity. Immediately, their defenses were lowered, and I was able to develop great relationships with them.

This was the script I used, which worked very well for me.

Hi _____, **I am so sorry** for not calling sooner. My name is _____. You left me a message about my opportunity. **How can I help you** _____?

Most of the time, they lower their guard right away and begin talking about why they called. At that point, you can politely ask them, "_(name)_, what changed in your life that made you decide to look into earning extra income?"

Offer to send some information and ask if you can follow up in about a week to see if they have any questions about the material. Consider calling them in between to invite them to any conference calls your company may be having. Don't use email to do this, because emails are impersonal. The information you send should include a cover letter introducing yourself and an offer to take action, as well as details about the opportunity. I like to use an offer of free postcards, leads, and placement in our team rotator for a period of time. Remember, people who respond to your ads are really asking for help, so reach out and offer that help.

What type of opportunity should I promote?

It really depends on your level of interest. Just make sure you do your research on the company. You may want to consider meeting the owner of the company in person or even get legal advice. Personally, I prefer health and wellness products because it's a billion-dollar industry and I'm a firm believer in nutrition. I'm also attracted to products that are consumable on a monthly basis because this helps create a steady monthly income. I look for products that are unique enough to be patented and this helps eliminate the competition. The overall financial health of the company is important too, as well as the compensation plan and type of products being offered. There are so many factors to consider and nobody can really predict the future. However, one thing is certain, network marketing can provide a decent income if done properly and I believe I've found the way.

Develop Leaders Who Duplicate

Your goal as a leader should be to develop leaders who duplicate your team concept. Network marketing is similar to playing Bingo; it's a numbers game. The more Bingo cards you play, the better your odds at winning. The more leaders you develop the more money you will earn. Encourage your team members to participate in your team concept and duplicate your system. Make sure you get written permission from the company and always follow their company guidelines and policies. If companies would embrace more of a team concept approach for their distributors, I believe it could have a positive impact as a whole.

If your passion is for helping others, then you are on the right track for building a successful network marketing business. People who are successful have one main thing in common, they never give up. Imagine the type of income you could earn in network marketing by just sharing your team concept with others. Ask yourself this question, are you motivated enough to help enough people get what they want, so you can get what you want? If the answer is yes, then work as a team, leverage, and duplicate your way to network marketing success.

***

To Contact Mark:

Cell: 260-804-4084

www.markrecker.com

Email: mrecker777@gmail.com

Team Website: www.JDILifeTeam.com

Facebook Page:
https://www.facebook.com/groups/TrueGlobalCompassion/?ref=bookmarks

Christian Fea

After surviving many career titles over the last 25 years in 22 different industries, I've come to the current conclusion that what I'm best known for and where I provide the most value to clients, business owners and entrepreneurs is in the *simplification of the complex*. Turning complex business problems into manageable, repeatable and scalable solutions are the areas of my greatest contributions. As a result of this type of thinking, progress and experience, the theme of *continual improvement strategist* came to be.

My journey of improvement and how things worked started at the age of 8, when I got my first computer. It was then, that I realized I had a fascination to not only understanding how the world worked, but more importantly, why things were done in a certain way. Understanding how you get from where you are now to where you'd like to be in the future, lead me towards a direction of research and experimentation of what was possible. By constantly asking questions of *why*, *how* and *what if,* led me toward the study of *process*, or breaking down large scale problems to its smallest unit of achievement.

Today, a large part of my contribution has been around making business processes easier, better and faster to produce a better outcome. Usually in the areas of sales, marketing, revenue generation and cost containment. Ultimately, through process improvement I've architected business systems that have allowed my clients to generate millions of dollars in sales and enjoy a more profitable, controllable and enjoyable business experience for their partners, investors, clients and employees.

The Empiring Productivity System

By Christian Fea

A productivity framework program designed for entrepreneurs for large scale achievement.

In its simplest explanation, Empiring is a framework that can enable you to double, triple or even quadruple your productivity in the areas you choose. It's a different way of approaching how you spend your time that's associated with your current and long term visions and objectives. A system to help you decide not only what projects and visions to invest your time on for your highest accomplishments, output or ROI, but also how to stay on course, execute effectively and how to course correct when you become unfocused and break momentum.

A bit of definition is in order before we progress. A *Vision is the ability to think about or plan for a future event with imagination or wisdom. A Goal is the object of a person's ambition or effort for a desired result.* As we progress through this chapter we're going to be using the word *Vision* as it relates to future projects, plans or our sought after outcomes. *Vision thinking* it's much more impactful and relevant in our study of large scale productivity and achievement. The key difference being a Vision has to do with imagination, which is free thinking and wisdom which is based on experience and progressive improvement.

The Empiring Framework is about continual achievement improvement in your areas of choice. It's designed to help you get from where you are now to where you want to be in a considerably reduced time cycle. While the Empiring Framework can be used in all areas of your life, including your relationships and personal adventures, for the context of this book, we'll be discussing how the Empiring Framework applies to your entrepreneurial venture. Starting a new business or growing an existing business.

When you study the top disciplines, leadership and management models of the last 25 year's certain patterns and benefits overlap.

Empiring is a hybrid model of these popular disciplines that extracts the core benefits of each discipline and takes into consideration the needs of an entrepreneur to simplify and reduce the time it takes to produce a successful outcome scenario, project, product, service or growth plan.

Here are a few of the existing disciplines that the Empiring Framework is based on:

Kaizen is the Japanese word for "improvement". Kaizen refers to activities that continually improve all areas of the business and insist on experience feedback from the entire business team. From the CEO to the mailroom clerk to the assembly line worker.

Scrum is a framework for project management that emphasizes teamwork, accountability and iterative progress toward a well-defined goal. The framework highlights a simple premise: Start with what can be seen or known and then track the progress and tweak as necessary.

Neo-Tech A series of extracted learnings from the richest Family Dynasties and the moguls of the industrial revolution. The basics of this discipline are *something more to life,* and discovering the *life you were meant to live.* Neo-Tech reveals how to unlock our bicameral mind from self-imposed, ask for permission, restrictive thinking (herd mentality) to integrated, self-guided, limitless thinking to create and build without limits.

Six Sigma is a disciplined, statistical-based, data-driven approach and continuous improvement methodology for eliminating defects in a product, process or service.

Root Cause Analysis is a problem solving methodology that focuses on resolving the underlying problem instead of a quick fix mentality that only treats an obvious and immediate symptoms of the problem. By asking *why* five times you get closer to discovering the true underlying problem.

The Empiring Framework can provide you with a feedback loop to help you breakdown the process of starting and growing your business. From initial concepts or ideas to breaking your inertia of what to work on next. Setting priorities, being mindful and removing wasteful habits and tasks, to building and sustaining momentum, handling challenges and setbacks. While the Empiring system is not a marketing, sales or business growth plan in itself, it's designed to sit on top of every marketing, sales, promotion, meeting and advertising program you engage in. Essentially it's the system you use to achieve your growth plans and keep you on top of your areas of purpose while you build and expand your business.

Overwhelm & Distraction

The daily roadblock to achievement

One of the biggest challenges that entrepreneurs face is the sheer volume of possibilities and opportunities that could be brought to fruition. Entrepreneurs tend to see the world differently than the average person or from an employee mentality. Entrepreneurs are builders, risk takers and dreamers, not maintainers of the status quo. The downside of *possibility intoxication* is the inevitable *decision fatigue* that sets in when constantly trying to decide where we should focus our time and energy for the greatest output or impact. With consistent confusion, over time, your speed of execution and momentum gradually decline until you actually start believing that what you're trying accomplish is so far out of reach that ultimately you may give up completely.

The Empiring system takes these vast *visions* and thoughts and breaks them down into manageable, linear *physical movements* to push through the confusion, excitement, fear and uncertainty that fills our mind when an idea or opportunity strikes us. Using *integrated thinking* to link or group similar actions together to accomplish more of the right projects can dramatically reduce time spent, resource dependency and monetary waste.

Projects of Impact

How to know what to work on

Another area of challenge in progressing your visions and achievements is not only knowing what to work on but what to prioritize. There are 4 primary psychological reasons for this that can present confusion and distraction in deciding what to work on:

It's satisfying to work on personal projects and ideas you'd use yourself, instead of projects with broad impact and reach.

It's tempting to focus on novel and clever ideas, instead of projects that directly impact your *visions*.

It's exciting to take on new ideas, rather than continue on projects that you've already started.

It's easy to underestimate the additional effort that one project will require over another.

Let's look at a popular project prioritization model called RICE. Which stands for reach, impact, confidence and effort.

Reach - The number of people your project could reach for a given project over a certain time period. For example, "How many customers will this project impact over a single quarter?"

Impact - To focus on projects that progress your goal, estimate the impact on an individual person. For example, "How much will this project increase our funnel conversion rate when a customer lands on it?"

Confidence - The percentage of confidence that a particular project will be completed based on the time, resources and focus available to you. 100% is *high confidence*, 80% is *medium*, 50% is *low*.

Effort - The estimated number of *person-months* of work that you or your team member can do in one month's time. This is rough estimate so use whole numbers and anything under 1 months of effort, use .5 as your multiplier. One month would be 1, 2 months would be 2, etc

So let's recap the whole process to figure out our RICE number for a given project.

RICE score = Reach x Impact x Confidence / Effort

Project	Reach	Impact	Confidence	Effort	RICE Score
Project 1	600	2	100%	4	300
Project 2	2900	1	80%	3	773
Project 3	300	3	50%	1	450

By using these simple calculations, you can start to remove personal bias, confusion and take a statistical approach to determine which *projects of impact* you could or should take action on.

Time Capture and Debunking the *busy* paradox

Your first Insight into how you're using your time resource - 24 * 30 * 12 * 79 = 682,560

Time, what is it? It's our only finite resource. Once it's gone, it's gone forever, we can't get it back. What does this formula mean? It's how many approximate hours we have in our lifetime. 24 hours in a day, 30 days per month, 12 months in a year and 79 years is the current average lifespan. The average age of a Man is 77 and a Woman is 81 years in the United States as of 2018. So *682,560 hours of time* is pretty much all we have to work with.

The first step towards understanding how you use time is to get a baseline understanding and document your current daily actions. Sound daunting, but it's not. It's actually very exciting to understand your time usage patterns. Warning! For most of you this process, maybe for the first time, will start to answer the question of *where does my time go?* This process of writing down everything you do from the time you get up in the morning until the time you go to bed is going to transform how you think about time. During this time logging exercise, you will start to visually see where, how and what you spend your time on, and understanding why the word *busy* and *productive* are unrelated. You can now better understand how to free up hours of wasted, random activity in your day to redirect this previously thought of *busy time* with far more productive plans.

Impulse Drifting

Understanding our constant stream of random thoughts.

According to current cognitive neuroscience research, we are aware of about 5 percent of our cognitive activity, so the vast majority of our decisions, actions, emotions, and behavior depends on the 95 percent of brain activity that goes beyond our conscious awareness.

In order to optimize or make something better you first have to come up with a baseline. Here's a listing of a single day of logged, high level activity. You should do this process for at least 3 days, but, ideally 7 days since your activities will be different on the weekend compared to the weekdays. This is an unoptimized listing of random actions that I've spent time on while allowing my mind to *impulse drift* or acting on impulse rather than planning an activity for a future point in time. This planning process as we'll see shortly is called *vision thinking* and *momentum buckets*. The below chart has no *integrated thinking*, not much planning, but pure consciousness followed by acting on that impulse. You can see by the activities in the below chart that while I seemed busy, I wasn't very productive and made very little progress towards my *projects of impact* due to the scattered nature of my day, just minor progress towards a project. Unfortunately, this is how most of us run our days. Day after day and this cycle continues for month and years to come. It no wonder we feel burnt out and dissatisfied with our achievements.

Date/Time	Impulse Drift Thought to Action	Time Spent
2019-02-28 6:45 AM	Blog article for May deadline	1.32
2019-02-28 8:45 AM	Talk with Mike on walk through project	2:00
2019-02-28 9:30 AM	Discovery Call w/Ralph	0:45
2019-02-28 10:30 AM	Purchase material for sales show on Amazon	1:00
2019-02-28 11:30 AM	Call Meredith on plan type and cancelation	1:00
2019-02-28 12:15 PM	Meet with James on CU updates	12:45
2019-02-28 12:21 PM	Break	0:06
2019-02-28 12:25 PM	Edits for Work Day project	0:04
2019-02-28 1:16 PM	Setup display ad marketing program	0:51
2019-02-28 2:47 PM	Importing past contacts for email campaign	1:31
2019-02-28 3:23 PM	Go to post office	0:36
2019-02-28 4:11 PM	Project updates with Simon	0:48
2019-02-28 5:15 PM	Call Matt on data format	1:04
2019-02-28 6:16 PM	Dinner with family	1:01
2019-02-28 7:05 PM	Kids and homework	0:49
2019-02-28 8:30 PM	TV & relax	1:25
2019-02-28 9:15 PM	Organize garage for movers this Friday	0:45
2019-02-28 10:45 PM	Prep for next day & sleep	1:30

While this list might look like a productive day, it really isn't for a number of reasons. First, these activities lack an area of purpose. The activities above are random thoughts of tasks that needed to be done, but not necessarily in the order or priority that I accomplished them during that day. An area of purpose from an entrepreneurial perspective could be a marketing program for example. An email marketing, content marketing, affiliate marketing, or a display ad marketing program. Something that can produce a profit. Now with every marketing or sales program, there are activities that equate to building and activities that equate to the tail of responsibilities that support the program. For example, when designing a display ad marketing program there are 8 steps that could go into this process. You need to:

Purchase credits on a display ad network

Configure the ad creative

Setup initial ads

Setup tracking analytics

A/B split test images, headlines, call to action variants

Determine conversion rates and ROI

Research other ad networks to replicate and scale

Repeat

You can see from my activity above at 1:16PM, I worked on 1/8th of my *area of purpose* to attempt to produce a profit. Hardly enough time and focus was allocated when you can see how much needs to be done for a successful program to come to fruition. Now you're starting to see how *impulse drifting* instead of integrated *area of purpose* thinking can wreak havoc on what gets accomplished over a period of time.

Compare the 1:16PM single task with what could have gotten done in one day compared to what actually got worked on in one day. A vast realization of un-optimized time that could of been spent focusing on the display ad marketing program to produce a profit. By fragmenting pieces of a project into multiple days and weeks and months, the probability of competing your *area of purpose* declines considerably. Inertia creeps in, you lose momentum and confidence in the project and other impulses, priorities and interruptions will come to mind to derail your focus.

Mind Capture

Capture your thoughts as they appear in your mind.

Our brains were not designed for conscious multi-step processing. In other words, the general consensus holds the belief that multitasking exists and that working on more than one task at a time produces a better or faster output. There are numerous, science backed research studies to support how multitasking is counterproductive in our quest for a successful, faster outcome.

I'll pull the curtain back on how the Empiring Framework evolves your projects and how I use it as an example. One of my *projects of impact* is this Empiring Framework. When ideas and thoughts come to mind, I don't act on them right away. I capture them as seen below, refine them, assign areas of purpose, physical movements and due dates. By looking at your captured thoughts in such a way, we reduce stress and repetitive thinking since we've captured the thought that we *eventually* want to work on. Now, we can begin to group these physical movements into time slots on a calendar which we call *momentum buckets*.

This tasks below represents an *integrated thinking* and grouping of associated *physical movements* and the area of purpose for each thought or task that you define as part of your *projects of impact*. We're going to assign due dates on our calendar that we'll associate to our *momentum buckets* in the next section.

Date Created	2019-02-22
Thought:	Every day you have the choice to be average or to be extraordinary
Purpose Tag:	thinkingBigProgram
Physical Movement:	Writing
Build/Maintain:	Build

Date Created	2019-02-23
Thought:	Write software expense audit for February 2019
Purpose Tag:	financialOptimizationProgram
Physical Movement:	Writing
Build/Maintain:	Build

Date Created	2019-02-24
Thought:	Call Insurance for enrollment update
Purpose Tag:	healthlyLivingProgram
Physical Movement:	Phone Call
Build/Maintain:	Maintain

Date Created	2019-02-25
Thought:	Goto Kinkos for passport picture
Purpose Tag:	travelProgram
Physical Movement:	Goto
Build/Maintain:	Build

Physical Movements

The smallest units of progress.

Productivity and achievement is about making consistent, daily progress towards your *projects of impact*. How do tasks, projects, goals and visions come to fruition? We've all heard dozens of times, "you must take action towards your objectives", but what is action and what type of action will bring you closer to your achievement in the least amount of time? Let's define an action as *the physical movement needed to advance your vision forward.* So what is a physical movement? It's 1 unit of a particular action. For example, from our display ad marketing program above. The first item on the list, *purchase credits on a display ad network.* That task by itself can be broken down into 3 units of action or 3 physical movements.

Research - Which network to use

Phone Call - Speak with someone in sales to answer your questions

Purchasing - Setup payment terms

The second task on our list is *configure the ad creative.* The physical movements for this task would be:

Meeting - With graphic designer to brainstorm ad ideas

Writing - Write headlines for display add based on brainstorming meeting

Design - Actually design the ad based on items 1 and 2 above

So my 1:16PM task being, *setup display ad marketing program*, which is actually a project, which is abstract, confusing and leads to many decisions needing to be made, which causes *decision fatigue.* We need to break it down to its core physical movements. Research, a phone call, purchasing, meeting and writing. These are straight forward, simple process based task units that don't require much brain power or investigation to produce progress towards your *projects of impact.* With this level of thinking your projects don't seem so daunting, abstract or out of reach. We all know what phone calls, meetings and writing entails. Confidence in thought breeds accomplishment in action. Now this is where it starts to get interesting since most of us have not been taught or practiced breaking down projects into this level of *physical movements.*

Momentum Buckets

Grouping your physical movements to time

We've seen from our Impulse Drifting exercise how our minds, if left to its own natural state has the repetitive tendency to pull us in many directions. Let's consider that we want to work a typical 10-hour day. If we extract out the *physical movements* and group them together into *Momentum Buckets* that add up to 100%, it would look something like this:

Phone Calls	20% - 2 hours
Writing	20% - 2 hours
Research	20% - 2 hours

Purchasing	10% - 1 hour
Meetings & People	20% - 2 hours
Design	10% - 1 hour

So we've allocated a certain amount of time for each physical movement and now we're going to allocate into groups called *Momentum Buckets. We're going to take these Momentum Buckets* and map them to time chunks on our calendar.

Phone Calls

7:00 - 8:50 AM

Call Bob about conference in NY

Call Sarah about onsite presentation

Call Mark about expanding territories in Chicago

Writing

9:00 - 10:50 AM

Write guest blog post for NY Times

Write 500 words on book project

Write email follow-up from trade show

Research

11:00 - 12:50 PM

Research latest insights on brain science

Research costs on display ad network

Research new influencers for affiliate program

Meetings & People

1:00 - 2:50 PM

Meet with Sean on email campaign to followers

Meet with Ann on copy for new website

Meet with Darius on new site features

Design

3:00 - 3:50 PM

Design new banner ad for A/B testing

Design new logo concept

Purchasing

4:00 - 4:50 PM

Purchase new paper samples for stationary project

Purchase credits for new ad network campaign

Purchase booth giveaway items from TSI

As you can see with the Empiring Framework, we can take multiple *projects of Impact*, break them down into their *physical movements* and group them together into their *Momentum Buckets* on our calendar. When you combine these 3 building blocks of progress, your productivity sores like never before. This framework allows you to take action on multiple *projects of impact* at once. Your confidence will rise, your stress will reduce and your overall sense of accomplishment will allow you to get more of right things done in a compressed time cycle than ever before.

Take Flight

Putting the pieces together.

As an entrepreneur, we're faced with a dizzying amount of decisions to make on a daily basis. Seeing the world as an endless opportunity, while exciting and fruitful, also come with a heavy time constraint. A question we frequently ask ourselves or should ask ourselves is, what's the best use of my time today for maximum return and ROI? We've touched on a few optimization methods to answer this question. We've also examined some of the core beliefs that may hold you back from achieving your *projects of impact*, making a difference or feeling empowered such as overwhelm and distraction. To correct this, we need to focus on our *areas of purpose* that group our actions together to stay focused and not allow our conscious minds to *Impulse Drift*. We learned how to capture our thoughts and convert them into *physical movements*, our basic building blocks of progress. By extracting the same physical movements over multiple projects and mapping those to our *momentum buckets* our productivity and feelings of accomplishment significantly increase. This allows us to propel past our once, self-imposed limited thinking, our competitors and break ground into new, vast areas of accomplishment you never thought possible along your journey of being an entrepreneur.

We've covered a tremendous amount of different types of thinking to propel and inspire you to higher levels of achievement in a far less amount of time. With this type of thinking comes many questions on how to best apply or adopt this into your daily habits and rituals. It's my sincere desire for you to expand your level thinking about what's possible and how to achieve it through the Empiring process planning framework. As a result, I've arranged for the readers of this book to get a free Empiring productivity session to help you implement the mindset and strategies that we've started to discuss in this chapter. The benefits and gains in productivity, in your feelings of confidence and beliefs of what's possible can be vastly more impactful than you ever thought possible. Imagine what's possible for yourself, your team and your close personal relationships! To claim your free Empiring productivity session, please go to: http://www.christianfea.com/richcode

***

To contact Christian:

https://www.linkedin.com/in/christianfea/

949-375-0215

christian@christianfea.com

Joy Gilfilen

Joy Gilfilen loves helping other trailblazers to successfully apply *The Joy Method: Proven Leadership Tools for Personal, Business and Civic Innovation.* By mastering her quantum leadership technologies, people reach a higher degree of achievement in their business, organization or community. Joy's models have been refined and honed over four decades of executive consulting and entrepreneurial experience.

Joy is the host of *JoyTalks* – a podcast series featuring community town halls where social activists work with business and civic leaders (inspired by free enterprise) to solve systemic community problems. These game-changing conversations reveal inherent fractures caused by system failures, homelessness, joblessness, poverty, mental health and drug addiction. Joy uncovers the local opportunities to transform these problems through sustainable living economies.

Joy has demonstrated a new way we can reform the jail industry with alternative health care solutions, new addiction recovery programs, apprenticeship programs, green living and new cooperative business situations.

Joy is an author, speaker, producer, trainer, and innovator. Joy's unique aptitude is helping groups of people rise above their differences, connect at heart and discover their own hidden resources and creative potential. This makes it possible for people to quantum leap seemingly insurmountable problems to experience the power of collaboration.

Quantum Leadership using the *Natural Change Model*

by Joy Gilfilen

Today, the world has become massively complex and is constantly in upheaval. What is the best code I can share to help you find your riches in the middle of chaos? How can I help you relate it to the current global opportunities we have to make a quantum shift as free, enterprising people working together? I can share what I know, the best way I know how.

Introducing the *Natural Change Model*

I built this model specifically to help myself thrive through this kind of situation. It worked, so I have taught others, and tested it in many different social and civic situations. I have found that it helps us:

- Maintain a "pivot foot" as we improve mental agility
- Learn to swivel, build resilience and strengthen our emotional core
- Learn to focus, move fast and change course as we desire
- Keep our feet on the ground as we break through resistance
- Stay on course to achieve our dreams under pressure
- Keep it simple, so we can easily expand and contract to meet demands
- Reduce barriers in communication to achieve more satisfying results

There was a time in the mid-90's that I was overwhelmed by the speed of change and the complexity in our world. I was feeling intense pressure to learn how to better deal with the size and scope of social, business, and civic problems. I led a multi-million dollar direct sales organization with 45 executives and over 5,000 customers in a national network. I had two young sons. My life was full. Too full.

The internet was barreling down on us. I had no idea how I was supposed to adapt to compound change. It was too much, too fast. I was a solo-entrepreneur with no technological background. I felt ill prepared and terrified. I knew it was going to hit like a tsunami.

In self-defense, I needed a way to cope. I started asking myself about the nature of change. How does it work? Was there any kind of universal agility pattern that could help me handle volumes? Was there anything that was lightweight, portable in my mind, that I could use anytime, anywhere to simplify my life and make managing so many variables easier?

As a young girl, my 'go to' safety net was to go talk with Mother Nature - to listen and observe. She handles the whole world in 365 day cycles. How does that work? Things are born, they die. There are tides, winds, weather. The sun comes up. The sun goes down. The moon comes up. The moon goes down. But in different cycles. Everything is changing 24/7. How does she do it? There has to be a simple pattern there somewhere.

I built myself a test model that works on natural cycles and applied it to managing complex business, family and civic situations. Its very simplicity makes it highly adaptive, useful and productive to use as a universal achievement agenda and field leadership tool. The better I am at using it, the faster and easier I get things done.

Natural Change Model: 5-Steps to Self-Leadership

This is a holistic systems model built for whole-brained thinking. It has a series of master principles that start from the simplest base where we reorient our minds to who we are as powerful, creative people. We expand in complexity as we grow outward. As we build in sequence, we combine thoughts to become a whole, the exponential sum of the working parts.

It starts with you. As I write this section, I will use the term "I" so you can feel the personal impact of this. I am you, the collective us. We are humans, similar to each other, yet uniquely different, and there are five basic dynamic moving forces at the foundation of this model. Who I am, how I work, how I live in context, what is changing now, and where I am going.

1. *Value – I am Human*: I am not just a body. I am an energy-generating powerful living human being with creative life force energy and influence that I can harness and direct like a laser. As an adult human being I am made up of 70 trillion replicating cells – and I am a quantum. I create, as well as react and respond to the changes around me in rhythms and waves.

2. *BodyMindSpirit* – **the Spiral of Life:** I am part of the composing and decomposing process of life itself. I have three integrated but different parts that we often call the Body, the Mind, and the Spirit. The Body is the physical, tangible, seeable or known part. The Mind is what is being currently created in a dynamic process. It is our mental world where things are being traded, negotiated, added together or taken apart like in physics or chemistry where we experiment with what we wish to create. The Spirit is the potential, the possibilities, the fuel, the intangible, divinely passionate part that inspires action to create form.

3. *Past-Present-Future Destination Map*: I am always going somewhere. From this view, I have a past, a present and a future that is always moving forward in the NOW. Being able to put the past behind me allows me to create a kind of superhighway, or a continuous pathway to achieve things. Think of it as a freeway. I use maps, charts, money, a compass, and various tools to help me on my journey. I set out milestones and goals to measure my progress. It is not so important to look in my rearview mirror as it is to look forward and keep my eye on the road ahead to reach my destination.

4. *Universal Chart of Constant Change*: This is a way of seeing myself above the NOW, so I can segment moving parts into a context of columns and lists from left to right. It allows me to see bi-directionally what is happening. I can see what's passing away or decomposing on my left. I can see what is currently now in the middle. I can see how life is bubbling up, emerging and composing on my right. I can then notice with objective awareness how I fit into the naturally evolving pattern of the greater decomposing and composing life cycle.

5. ***Values-to-Vision Compression Process***: Nothing moves dynamically until I have emotionally empowered my vision. Everything grows from my own foundation of core ***Values*** and focus towards ***Vision***. It moves in undulating spiral motion and rhythmic cycles of repeating BodyMindSpirit waves. This motion is harnessed (compelled, propelled and inspired) by my own choices, and by the actions, reactions and desires of life itself. The spark, the impetus to take action, is fueled by the expanding fire in my belly.

The desire to achieve that vision is the ignition control switch that turns up the power of my life. It's the activating force that makes everything move. It ignites and launches our internal combustion chamber where joy resides. Joy is activated by the bubble-up of enthusiasm seeking its visionary manifestation. Joy is the energy that dissolves and eradicates fear.

The more joy I have inside, the more I work in the BodyMindSpirit dynamic world. Then the faster my creative juices flow into a sequence of reactions that increase power in that piston pump system. My pump produces and amplifies power to achieve my vision. I become like a drill bit of human power that moves through the universe to achieve my dreams.

The *Fear to Joy Gauge*: Putting Concepts into Action

This *Natural Change Model* is a basic self-renewing sequence. Similar to how a powerful engine works in a race car. The idea is ignited, and then develops into form and function. I use it for managing myself, coaching others. I use it in planning, for dissecting a problem to find solutions, and predicting trends. I use it to pack for a vacation, or to organize a group of diverse people to accomplish something grand.

Once I fully understand 1) how my personal values establish my innate power as a human, and 2) that I am a proactive creative being, then it changes my perception about how the world works. I learned to use my whole brained energy to focus my power differently. I realized my third eye serves as a laser beam, like a telescope I can adjust, and as a camera where I can change lens at will.

With this visionary viewfinder in my third eye I open and close apertures, change lens, put in overlays and use different navigation tools at will. It makes it easier to see bigger, scarier, and more complex images without being afraid or overwhelmed. I can sort, clarify, reduce and expand, prioritize and focus on different goals more easily.

The question becomes, "What riches do I circulate, share, assimilate, put forth, and create that generate positive feelings and satisfaction?"

A different set of navigation tools is exposed. One specifically is an emotional guidance system, similar to a speedometer or compass in a car. It is my emotional gyroscope, or sniffer detector. It is a tool that tells me if I am on or off course.

This *Fear to Joy Gauge* has a needle that points to the left, the middle or right.

If the needle is pointing to the far left, it is red-lining. It indicates fear, resistance, and constriction. It indicates I might be holding on to the past, might be avoiding change, or I might need to shift gears. If the needle is not pointing too far left, I use the past as a resource and reference.

If the needle is in the center, with the point up, I register calmness of love in the present. It reflects my comfort with normal as the world ebbs and flows. I absorb and feel peace in the space between the past and the future.

If the needle is pointing more to the right, I am engaging my vision and inner joy to build my future actively. This shows substantial energy developed and harnessed to propel action.

If the needle goes too far right, I redline. I burn too much energy which is unsustainable.

Understanding Converging Power and Ripple Effects

I've learned to see my part in the living world, an interconnected being in the global sea of life. However tiny my part, I have a direct circle of influence where I make a difference.

Every human is powerful human being. You, too impact and make waves within your own circle of influence. You cause a ripple effect, which can magnify over time.

We each live in different industry sectors, and these sectors transform, collide and converge. Families and communities evolve in leaps and bounds. We impact each other in our personal sphere.

As we team up across sectors we bring our talents and resources to bear and create larger circles of influence. As we merge, we compound our power and effectiveness to achieve greater results.

To be effective, however, we must comprehend the complexity and size of the current crisis we face. Working as a team, we expand our collective viewfinder.

As we uncover the scope of the challenges, it allows us to find extraordinary opportunities.

- Our global outer world is changing fast. As noted in the daily news, entire countries and global systems are deep in tumult, wars, disasters, and serious climate change.
- In the US our institutions, systems and financial markets are in a quagmire of chaos. Excessive government and quasi-government corporations hold taxpayers hostage to political gamesmanship.
- People feel extreme distress by the economic inequities as the middle class loses ground. The poor are dealing with the repetitive impacts of generational poverty, incarceration, and bias which cause complex social trauma, mental distress, and addictive behaviors.

In this downward spiral there is opportunity to work together as local entrepreneurs and small businesses. We can change the tide. In the past, we have allowed the government to become top heavy. We have allowed huge global corporations to control entire market sectors. We have allowed people to be traumatized and misused by systems that are not self-correcting. This means our communities have been hemorrhaging money to large multi-national corporations who have been marginalizing local business.

The past does not equal the future. It is time for us in local communities to take back our economic power.

The Great Opportunity: When Enterprising People Team Up with Vision!

Working together in new ways we can create self-renewing local living economies. We can implement new restorative economic models. We can invest in sustainable business practices. We can discover new innovative technologies; repair the immune systems and health of our earth, ourselves, our friends and neighbors.

It is time for a profound small business transformation and for free enterprise revolution. People around the world working in small pods have already developed ways to restore social, structural and systemic integrity. We can expand on that knowledge. Yes, it will take work and this is the greatest skill of trailblazers and entrepreneurs. When we stop living into our past fears and historic failures we can change habits. We naturally pivot toward a world that revitalizes right-sizes and rebalances our land and people.
This enriches compassion, creativity, collaboration and construction of things shared within a group.

The good news is that none of this is a stretch for local enterprising people. People naturally team up in small pods and network across the nation using social media. Knowledge expands as we learn from other smart people in other smart communities.

We evolve into a new world where we can identify and upgrade our local community business models to perform at a higher level while being responsive to local needs. This brings financial riches and strengthens emotional, regenerative community wealth.

How You Can Implement the *Natural Change Model* in Your Business

1. *Value – I am Human*: Respect the power and value in yourself and those around you. Value the abilities and diverse experiences of the people in your community, county, state, region. Allow people to participate and contribute according to their ability. We all desire to have a voice and contribute meaning. Welcome new ideas and appreciate individual contributions.

2. *BodyMindSpirit* – **The Spiral of Life:** Monitor the health and structure of the physical, tangible parts of your business for viability and sustainability. Maintain mental agility and adaptability to trends, conditions and opportunities. Be on the lookout for new information and viewpoints. Understand your motivation, inspiration and passion. Allow your vision and potential to evolve, and communicate clearly to inspire others into action. Cultivate these three parts in balance with each other.

3. **Your** *Past-Present-Future Destination Map:* Map out the complexity of the past, present, and future of your business, your colleagues, your community. Identify your benchmarks, review your outcomes and set new goals. Be aware that your destination may change as you proceed along your journey. Refresh your Past-Present-Future periodically to celebrate your achievements. Adjust goals affected by changes in your community or marketplace.

4. *Universal Chart of Constant Change*: Identify your position in relation to the bigger picture. Create a 3-column chart that reflects the Past, the Present and the Future. Quantify the differences among the social, economic and civic shifts that affect your business. Revise and update this chart as current events transpire. This helps you see the part you play in the larger context, and provides clues to where you can make a difference, and identifies potential partners and allies.

5. *Values- to-Vision Compression Process*: Galvanizing your core values into a cohesive movement towards your larger vision attracts collaborators who share those same values. This brings in diverse points of view, enriches the field of opportunity for new ideas to incubate, and businesses to flourish. The exponential power will grow your impact as it ripples outward in your local economy, which inspires others to expand solutions and achieve results.

Through the rich human power of collaborative hearts, minds and spirit we unite with the natural rhythms and flows of life to rebuild our communities from the ground up. There are millions of seeds planted within our networks waiting to be nourished. I believe that the freedom loving, enterprising people of today have the resources and knowledge to enrich our individual capacity to bear fruit. Our mutual prosperity flows from the synergistic networks of people working together in harmony, inspiring joy and happiness. Circulation is the inner nature of abundance.

***

Main Site: joygilfilen.com

Products: joygilfilen.com/thejoymethod

Subscribe to: patreon.com/joygilfilen

Friend at: https://www.facebook.com/joygilfilen

Follow at: https://www.facebook.com/votingforjoy

Network at: https://www.linkedin.com/in/joygilfilen

Non-Profit Project: therestorativecommunity.org

Mache Torres - Ackerman

Mache is an educator, entrepreneur, international author, transformational life coach, socio-civic leader and a philanthropist.

She is a co-owner of the family-owned business, St. James College System. St. James is a 48-year old private educational institution founded by her parents: the late Jaime T. Torres and Myrna Montealegre-Torres.

As an entrepreneur, she is the co-founder of Triumphus Inc. Fuel Experts which deals with wholesale and retail of Petroleum Products and founder of Triumphus Estates, Inc., a real estate development company.

As an international certified life coach and hypnotherapist who is best known to unleash one's fullest potential ...

As a philanthropist and a socio-civic leader, she is the founder of Mache Torres Advocacy and Leadership Programs Inc. & (TASA) -Transformational Advocacy Thru Self Awareness. She has done countless outreach activities as the Charter President of Rotary Club of Makati Business District, Philippines.

She is a co-author of THE CHANGE Book Series - 8 & 10, launched in the US, together with top international authors and power speakers Jim Britt & Jim Lutes. She is the author of "So Near Yet So Far." "Explore The Deepest Essence of Your Being" and her upcoming book "You Are Brand New!" which will be launched soon.

Mache is blessed with five beautiful daughters namely: Mica; Bea; Cielo; Daniela and Emilia.

Transformational Entrepreneurship for Sustainability Thru Spirituality and Self Mastery

By Mache Torres - Ackerman

Transformational leadership is a challenging task to most entrepreneurs. This chapter was written with the same challenge and struggle for me since I will be citing my family business as a case study on this issue.

I grew up in a family with enterprising parents. A power couple indeed! My father was a successful customs broker and my mom was a passionate educator. After they got married, my dad asked my mom to retire as a school teacher from a prestigious school and to be a stay-at-home mom while he continues his customs brokerage business.

My mother as a true educator with a passionate heart -- obviously got bored and started a pre-school business as a hobby. My dad, being a visionary and a natural entrepreneur, saw the potential of her business and expanded it. It was hard to envision the business in a country wherein schools were mostly run by the religious sectors, hence they viewed it as a non-profit institution.

Together as co-founders, they expanded the school into several branches: from kindergarten, elementary, secondary, and up to the collegiate levels! Their partnership was complimentary and was so inspiring. Both of them came from humble beginnings, and as achievers, they managed to keep their feet on the ground empowered by their deep sense of faith and spirituality. I was brought up and was trained to face struggles and trials through patience, perseverance and prayers.

I literally grew up with the business and was mentored by both my parents. I was trained and mentored by example. They both possessed a kind of leadership that inspired employees to help the business grow. I was trained to always look at the bigger picture and to appreciate the positive side of any situation. I saw how the schools expanded into several branches and how it became a school system.

My father taught me that counting profit is not enough. It is all about reinvesting your gains. He was a visionary and invested in real estate which amplified the company's net worth and assets.

Through my parents I learned that,

Entrepreneurship is about passion! Do what you are passionate about and you will never have a day of work. I have seen both my parents as passionate individuals who have pursued their purposes in life together. They both had humble beginnings and they know how to give back to the society through philanthropic deeds. Our family has formed a foundation that has granted scholarships to thousands of students who are now successful in their own fields.

However, it was not a perfect world after all. When my father passed away, we were forced to deal with the reality of our family dynamics. I have four siblings and the five of us had to deal with each other and our mother who had to face her own inner struggles.

After almost fifty years of our family's legacy, we had to let go and face the reality. Due to the family feud and power struggles, the business suffered. As a family, we have to accept, we have to let go! It is not easy and we know that the students and alumni feel the loss. Although it is the best move, to move on individually and reinvent ourselves. After all, my father's legacy lives in my heart, and I thank him for all the learnings!

KEYS TO SUSTAINABILITY THRU TRANSFORMATIONAL ENTREPRENEURSHIP

Have an advocacy thru Social Entrepreneurship

Living in a developing country like the Philippines, us entrepreneurs belong to the upper bracket of the society. We are programmed to give back to the society and to help out communities. We support government and non-government organizations as part of our CSR -Corporate Social Responsibility.

Having a specific advocacy aside from profit earning is called social entrepreneurship. Apart from gaining profit from a place of substance, having a business in this model just as well adds ethical value and an automatic unique selling point.

Keep your integrity intact

A lot of business individuals are so focused on profit making without considering other aspects. I have seen many businesses grow fast, but quickly failed due to lack of integrity.

As an active civic leader and a member of Rotary International (an international business and service organization www.rotary.org), I am guided by integrity in business and relationships through the Rotary Four Way Test: 1. Is it the truth? 2. Is it fair to all concerned? 3. Will it build goodwill and better friendships? 4. Will it be beneficial to all concerned?

I have grown up being taught the universal rule as well: "Don't do unto others what you don't want others to do unto you".

Lead yourself first before others – SELF LEADERSHIP

As I quote myself from my other book, "Self-leadership is a pre-requisite to organizational leadership." (THE CHANGE BOOK 10 SERIES) Everything definitely starts from the self! In any endeavour that one partakes, it is important to make sure that one's internal issues are intact. Having inner peace is necessary to be able to maximize one's potential which in effect can easily inspire others (i.e. business partners; employees.) At the same token, a person or a leader with inner peace can easily have a compassionate soul. A compassionate heart can easily connect with people. A people person is an inspiring leader who can empower and maximize his/her employees' potential as well.

Our educational institution had at least 500 employees. It was not easy to lead a huge organization unless you can easily connect with your people. Self-mastery leads to people mastery. One of the weaknesses that caused the downfall was when the new management could not empower the right leaders. There was no proper motivation that lead to bad service and lack of the usual enthusiasm to run the business.

The culture drastically changed. The management and the employees had a misaligned mission and vision which weakened the usual foundation.

Be curious and hungry for knowledge

We are never too old to learn! Education is a lifelong process which should enhance our curiosity to know more. Curious children are smart children. That is the reason why parents are expected to be very patient when answering all of their child's queries. Their subconscious minds are like sponges that absorb all the everyday learnings from everyone (their parents; teachers; friends; social media). As adults, maximizing our own subconscious minds is just as important. A lot of people are trapped with the old saying, "You can never teach old dogs new tricks!". Wrong!!! If we think of ourselves as that, then we can never adapt to change. *Sometimes,* we *even* need to unlearn in order to relearn. With the current fast paced society, it would be difficult to sustain a business without adapting to the changing times.

I am still struggling to finish my doctorate degree due to my hectic schedule. But I promised myself to keep on trying until I achieve my goal. As I reinvent myself, I am open to knowledge and explore different fields.

Be open to CHANGE!

Change is the only thing that is constant in this world! Successful industries are subjected through constant change and development due to evolving trends in the market. As a result, continuous market and product research is necessary to keep up with the fast pace of the growing economy. A person who is not adaptable to change is incapable to growth. That is the reason why entrepreneurs are flexible individuals.

One of the downfalls of most institutions is the lack of openness to change. A common perspective in Development Studies is the concept of the Modernization Theory; wherein true development cannot be achieved through sticking with tradition and old ideologies, rather, it is achieved through the innovation of new concepts and ideologies (Goorah, 2010).

Many founders think that what worked before can always work over time. It is a common perceived ego of founders to say "I did it my way!". Sadly, most family-owned empires are short lived without successfully being succeeded by the third generation due to the differences in leadership style.

All persons have within them the power to change the conditions of their lives. Higher vibrations consume and transform lower ones; thus, each of us can change the energies in our lives by understanding the Universal Laws and applying the principles in such a way as to effect change.

Have a proper Succession Management

Lack of succession management is another common downfall in any business or a family-owned enterprise. The founders are trapped in their own realities, beliefs, and egos. The "old school" ways may have worked during their founding years, but as time progresses, development must also happen. This is why resiliency is important. The second generation owners are the ones who take the challenge of a huge transition without readiness.

Typical family dynamics that get in the way are the following: fear of change by the founders; succession to the unqualified child due to favouritism over expertise; lack of trust and fear of letting go due to inner struggles / insecurities; and power struggle and control.

My father was not ready to let go even if he was diagnosed with liver cancer. Our family had high hopes of his fullest recovery after his successful liver operation. It was just unfortunate that due to internal stress he had a massive stroke that caused his sudden death.

My mother who is a co-founder could not let go as well and due to her personal issues and internal struggles, she empowered the unqualified heir to run the business which lead to its downfall.

Learn from the past

The start of real change is acceptance of failure. Not all successful entrepreneurs started with a perfect business model. Most of the biggest industries in the market learned from "trial and error". Most entrepreneurs are so passionate with their ideas that they do not take the time to do their market research. Although after implementing a product or a conceived idea, they are open to adjusting to the market's needs and changes of the times. They have the natural capacity to adjust and reinvent their products or services.

Introspection of oneself is just as important. How did I handle a situation that lead to failure? Why did my employee react negatively towards me? How can I improve on my product/ service?

Have a global mentality

On this day and age, entrepreneurs have a global perspective. It is now easier for younger entrepreneurs to make global connections due to technological advancements. I still vividly remember my father decades ago when he would hand write his simple memorandums to the employees, then his assistant would type it for him. After that, he would still have to ask them to retype every correction made. Looking back, there was so much effort and time consumed as compared to using laptops, tablets, and mobile phones nowadays. All sorts of documents can be shared now using iCloud, email, and Bluetooth!

Even meetings nowadays are more productive! Online conference calls have also risen in popularity that travelling is not as necessary unlike decades ago.

This book is a perfect example of global-mindfulness wherein we are collaborated authors from around the world sharing our own thoughts and expertise.

Consider advancement thru networking

There are several business international organizations nowadays that are actively connecting people of similar industries. It is important to connect and to actively participate as an entrepreneur in order to be updated. I myself attend all the available talks and conferences that interests my passion and line of expertise.

I grew up attending international conferences for educators with both my parents as my bosses. As young as early twenties, I have met the most successful educators; administrators and school business owners from across the globe. I learned a lot from them and until now I am actively attending talks and seminars. With that, I have witnessed the changes throughout the years. After meeting important business icons decades ago, it was difficult to reconnect without travelling back to their countries. Nowadays, the power of social media has made it easier to stay connected and to build more business relationships.

Let energies be at work, learn how to work with your energy!

Everything around us is energy! A successful entrepreneur knows how to maximize one's energy and potential. Positive manifestation is as important as setting your own goals. It is energy at work putting your visions into reality. As we positively charge ourselves in a holistic way: mentally; physically; emotionally; and spiritually, we easily attract the right people in the right place and time. Opportunities open and we are made to be in a "state of knowing". Decision making becomes faster and it feels right!

Have a benchmark for success!

Goal-oriented entrepreneurs have a benchmark for success! I personally update myself on the Forbes yearly top list for inspiration. It is important to know who are the top players of each field so we can learn from them and be inspired by them.

I consider myself lucky for being surrounded in a circle of successful business icons whom I consider as my mentors.

Have the humility to seek mentorship

Part of success is knowing your own strengths and weaknesses. Having the humility to accept your weaknesses and asking for mentorship is part of the formula. My father was mentored by his senior colleagues and I have met tycoons who were mentored by other tycoons as well.

Sometimes we do not need to go thru the process to learn. Mentors can inspire and teach us thru their own experiences that can save us from the troubles. They have been there and done that so they are considered credible teachers.

Deal with your Inner conflict thru forgiveness

Aside from dealing with my inner struggles for the past decade, wherein I had to heal myself from a failed marriage, I also had to face an internal conflict within the family that affected our family business. The loss of our father, as our patriarch and founder, rocked the entire ship! We had to all deal with power struggle and control.

There was no way to go but to let go and to let God! Without my intense faith and hope, I could not have kept my sanity. I owe it all to my Higher Power who guided and provided me with internal healing and strength to move on.

I learned to forgive myself and others. Unloading of the painful and negative past renewed my life, as I have let go of childhood issues and my failed marriage traumas as well.

Define your own purpose

I had to reinvent myself and to follow my calling and purpose in life. Aside from being a real estate entrepreneur, I am actively pursuing my purpose as a transformational life coach. After all my trials and tribulations in life, I have discovered my gift to empower and heal others after going thru the process as well.

Living in a country that is going thru a huge transition, I am pursuing my advocacy to empower women, fight drugs and corruption by sharing my expertise with training modules and seminars that enhances self-mastery for self-improvement.

Let go and let God!

Trusting our higher power empowers us spiritually! Spiritual leadership is becoming more popular especially in our country that has gone through and is still going through transformation and healing. Not everyone is ready to go thru the process due to delayed learnings of some leaders and individuals.

In this coming decade, people should look beyond the traditional business mindset. But instead to focus on the bigger picture, by accepting our calling, working on our inner strength for the sustainable success of our industries.

Make a difference!

True legacy and success are achieved when you can make a difference! It just feels fulfilling that a lot of students and scholars from our schools are more than grateful to our family. My personal prayer is: "God please help me achieve absolute prosperity so I can give much more back to others…"

I have reinvented myself thru self- mastery which made me more aware of who I really am and what I am supposed to do in this lifetime.

Hence, I conclude that transformational entrepreneurship is truly vital for sustainability and advancement thru deep spirituality and self-mastery.

I am grateful to the universe for all the learnings and blessings!

***

To contact Mache:

Website: www.machetorres.com

Skype: mache888

Mobile/ Viber / Whatsapp: 63 917 5940412

Email: machetorres412@yahoo.com

Facebook: Mache Torres Advocacy & Leadership Programs Inc.

Afterword

Life and business is always a series of transitions… people, places, and things that shape who we are as individuals. Often, you never know that the next catalyst for improving your business and life is around the corner, in the next person you meet or the next book you read.

Jim Britt, Kevin Harrington and Joel Sauceda have spent decades influencing individuals and entrepreneurs with strategies to grow their business, developing the right mindset and mental toughness to thrive in today's business environment and to live a better life.

Allow all you have read in this book to create a new you, to reinvent yourself and your business model if required, because every business and life level requires a different you. It's your journey to craft.

Cracking the Rich Code is a series that offers much more than a book. It's a community of like-minded influencers from around the world. A global movement. Each chapter is like opening a surprise gift, that just may contain the one idea that changes everything for you. Watch for future releases and add them to your collection. If you know of anyone who would like to be considered as a co-author for a future volume, have them email our offices at support@jimbritt.com

The individual and combined works of Jim Britt, Kevin Harrington and Joel Sauceda have filled seminar rooms to maximum capacity and created a worldwide demand. If you get the opportunity to attend one of their live events, jump at the chance. You'll be glad you did.

If you are an entrepreneur and would like to get the details about becoming a coauthor in the next Cracking the Rich Code book in the series, contact Jim Britt at jimbritt@jimbritt.com.

To Schedule Jim Britt, Kevin Harrington or Joel Sauceda as a featured speaker at your next convention or special event, email: support@jimbritt.com

Master your moment as they become hours that become days.

Make it a great life!

Your legacy awaits.

STAY IN TOUCH WITH JIM, KEVIN AND JOEL

For daily strategies and insights from top entrepreneurs, join us at

THE RICH CODE CLUB

FREE members site.

www.TheRichCodeClub.com

www.ingramcontent.com/pod-product-compliance
Lightning Source LLC
Chambersburg PA
CBHW071158210326
41597CB00016B/1596